Walking
ON

Walking ON

A Daughter's Journey with Legendary Sheriff Buford Pusser

By Dwana Pusser

With Ken Beck and Jim Clark

PELICAN PUBLISHING COMPANY
GRETNA 2009

*The word "Pelican" and the depiction of a pelican
are trademarks of Pelican Publishing Company, Inc.,
and are registered in the U.S. Patent and Trademark Office.*

Library of Congress Cataloging-in-Publication Data

Pusser, Dwana.
  Walking on : a daughter's journey with legendary sheriff Buford Pusser /
by Dwana Pusser with Ken Beck and Jim Clark.
    p. cm.
  ISBN 978-1-58980-583-5 (hardcover : alk. paper) 1. Pusser, Buford,
1937- 2. Sheriffs—Tennessee—Biography. 3. Pusser, Dwana. 4. Fathers
and daughters. I. Title.
  HV7911.P85P87 2008
  363.2092—dc22
  [B]

                          2008023718

Printed in the United States of America
Published by Pelican Publishing Company, Inc.
1000 Burmaster Street, Gretna, Louisiana 70053

To my parents, Buford and Pauline Pusser, who brought me into this journey, and to my daughters, Atoyia and Madison, who I hope will continue the legacy of Walking On

Contents

Preface

For there to be heroes in this world, there must be villains. The American South has had its share of both.

In 1937, when the Great Depression was still gripping the nation, my daddy, Buford Pusser, was born in McNairy County in southwest Tennessee. Times were tough, but Daddy's family worked hard and patched together a decent livelihood and life for themselves.

In the wake of World War II and on the brink of racial turmoil, Vietnam, and assassinations that would soon tear at the nation, life showed signs of becoming less harsh for folks in just about all corners of the country, including McNairy County. By the late 1950s and early 1960s, a small economic boom was under way along the Tennessee-Mississippi state line between McNairy and Alcorn counties.

With that relative prosperity came a sinister invasion by some very bad people. Many of these evildoers had been chased out of Phenix City, Alabama, a place nicknamed "Sin City" by the soldiers of World War II stationed at Fort Benning, Georgia. The criminals ruling Phenix City proved ruthless as they preyed upon G.I.s and their families—so much so that Gen. George S. Patton grumbled that he might have to move his tanks across the Chattahoochee River and "mash Phenix City flat."

After the assassination of attorney general-elect Albert Patterson in 1954, the governor of Alabama declared martial law and put the National Guard in charge of the battle to rid the town of its gangsters and other career criminals.

Rooting out perpetrators of crimes ranging from prostitution, bribery, and murder to gambling, robbery, and bombings, the National Guard made hundreds of arrests that led to almost as many convictions, including those of prominent politicians and law-enforcement officers.

During the cleansing of Phenix City, some of the mob scurried off to the area just above Corinth, Mississippi, and below Selmer, Tennessee, right along the state line. By the late 1950s, criminals ruled this corridor and made life miserable for locals and for travelers who stopped by for a meal or a good night's sleep—or maybe for what they thought would be some harmless "action."

The mile-long stretch of U.S. Highway 45 at the border was riddled with dangerous motels, restaurants, and taverns where you could buy just about anything—legal or illegal. If you made the mistake of flashing too much cash, the odds were good that you'd never see the next sunrise. And it was just as certain that your body would never be found.

Even though both state line counties were dry, sales of illegal alcohol flowed as freely as the nearby Tennessee River, which was reputed to be the final resting place for many missing victims of the state line thugs. For decades, the state line was infected with this epidemic of crime similar to what had plagued Phenix City. It was also where hit men and other hoodlums from as far away as Chicago and New York came to lie low and avoid the law.

It was into this setting that Daddy returned home as a young man in 1956 after an abbreviated stint in the Marines. His first confrontation with the notorious mob left an unhealable scar in his memory and hardened his dedication to stamp out these enemies of his home and way of life.

As McNairy County sheriff from 1964 to 1970, Daddy began a crusade that shut down the area's illegal alcohol trade, the backbone of the organized crime that was gnawing its way into every aspect of decent living. He knocked out scores of moonshine stills and put a slew of bootleggers, thieves, and violent men behind bars.

His biggest enemies were the state line criminals, in

particular Louise Hathcock and Carl ("Towhead") White, who considered himself the "Al Capone of the South." Daddy pursued the state line villains with a vengeance equal to the crooks' lust for power and wealth. Considered by some to be a vigilante cop, Daddy had numerous attempts made on his life. By the time his war on crime was over, Hathcock and White would be dead, and Daddy would lose his wife—my mother—to cold-blooded ambushers.

Through it all, my daddy walked tall and stood firm. And when required, he came ready to swing a big stick.

Acknowledgments

It has taken me quite a while to write this book. Many times I thought it would be too painful, but then I found a lot of joy remembering the good times of my childhood along with the bad times. Without key people in my life, I would not be the person I am today. I wish to thank those people:

My aunt Gail, who was the best aunt a girl could ever have. It was just us for many years.

James and Norma Wood, for their love and guidance.

My daddy's good friend, Jack Coffman, who helped me in telling the great stories, and his other wonderful friends, who assisted with this project: Bill Wagner, Juanita Richardson, Paul Wallace Plunk, Roger Horton, Billy Frank Harris, Don Browder, and Rod Provience.

Steve and Sherry Sweat, for promoting the Buford Pusser legacy and helping keep my dad's story alive. And Steve for his historical knowledge.

My manager Rex Robinson, attorney Terry Wood, and sidekick Shirley Sparks, a.k.a. Mama Shirley. Thanks for trying to keep me straight in business and in life. Also Rex, for his welcome input on the book.

My brother by heart, Ronald Hardin. Just know that you and your parents have meant the world to me.

Mel Carnal, who gave me what was really my first great job and who was a mentor to me during the sixteen years of my radio career.

Becky and Jim Kerr, who gave me guidance and became my "Savannah family" when I moved to Savannah, Tennessee.

Those who work now or have worked at the Buford Pusser Museum, for the great job they have done and continue to do in helping tell Daddy's story.

Dr. James Spruill and Dr. John Vinson, for keeping me on my feet and in the right frame of mind with this crazy disease called multiple sclerosis. They both helped me more than they know.

Wiley Brewer, for his wonderful photography work for this book and the museum.

Ken Beck and Jim Clark, for the tireless hours, weeks, and years that they put in this book. Thank you for keeping me going on this project.

My family. Thank you for your love and support.

Finally, my daughters, Atoyia and Madison, for their unconditional faith and love. Always remember you had a wonderful grandfather who would have loved to have gotten to know you. And my grandson, Hayse. You're your great-grandfather's namesake. Walk tall, son, and be proud.

—Dwana Pusser

In addition to all the folks above, we would like to thank Ken's wife, Wendy, and daughter and son, Kylie and Cole; Jim's wife, Mary; and Peggy Evans, John Seigenthaler, Al Knight, Drew White, Brent Baldwin, and Glenda Washam.

—Ken Beck and Jim Clark

Introduction

If anybody ought to be crazy, it's me.

We have Western Mental Health Institute over in Bolivar, Tennessee, not far from where I live. It's where they send crazy folks from our part of the state. I've told people that I could have been locked up at Bolivar a long time ago. If the people I'm telling that to don't know me very well, they just look at me like I'm talking crazy. If they know me well enough, though, they just shake their heads and sigh.

My mother was murdered in an ambush when I was six years old. My father died in my arms when I was thirteen. All I have to do is start telling my life story. If that doesn't get me a lifetime pass to Bolivar, then nobody else should be there at all.

My daddy was Buford Pusser. After graduating from high school, he joined the Marines and later went to Chicago to work and attend mortuary school. While there, he became a professional wrestler. Because of his size—six foot six and weighing in at 250 pounds—they nicknamed him "Buford the Bull."

It was because of his wrestling that he met and married my mother in 1959. I was born in Chicago in 1961 but moved to my daddy's hometown of Adamsville, Tennessee, with my family when I was an infant. Daddy became police chief of Adamsville and then sheriff of McNairy County. His exploits were turned into a hit motion picture in 1973 called *Walking Tall*. One of the most dramatic scenes in the

15

movie was the ambush of my parents by mobsters that resulted in the death of my mother.

Daddy's life was made into a film because he was larger than life. The film turned him into a legend, but even the film, which of course had plenty of fictional elements, couldn't capture the complexity of the real man behind both the legend and the character on the silver screen.

Daddy was most famous for tearing up stills and busting up disreputable joints, but he was the kind of man who didn't go looking for trouble. On the other hand, if it came to him, he didn't back away from it. In his six years as sheriff of McNairy County, he killed two people in self-defense. He was stabbed seven times and shot eight times. He more than held his own when he got into a fight with six men at once. He sent three of them to the hospital. The other three went to jail.

But there was another side to him that was more like a gentle giant.

My daddy was everything to me. He was my whole world. He was not only my father. Sometimes he was my mother. He also was my best friend.

My daddy, Buford Hayse Pusser, was only thirty-six years old when he died. This is the story of his life and my life—with and without my father.

I'll share my theory about why I think the wreck that killed my father was not an accident. To support my theory, I will reveal astonishing documentation never before published. In fact, only a few people know that the documentation exists, and only a handful have actually seen it—until now.

After I've finished telling what I know, I hope you'll feel like you know my daddy and me. Maybe you'll think I'm just talking crazy.

Maybe you'll just shake your head and sigh.

Walking
ON

CHAPTER 1

My First Memories and Early Childhood

My earliest memories are from the time our family lived in a little trailer out on Maple Street in Adamsville, Tennessee. I remember one time I had been really sick. I couldn't have been more than three years old. I believe Daddy was not yet county sheriff but was still police chief of Adamsville. My parents had taken me to see Dr. Wallace Vinson, who was our family doctor. Throughout my daddy's life in law enforcement, Dr. Vinson would be a central figure.

Dr. Vinson prescribed some cough medicine for me, and my parents gave me a dose when we got home. It was cherry flavored and evidently must have had a lot of sugar in it because I really liked it. I remember that my daddy was in the living room with my older stepbrother, Mike. They were down on the floor playing a board game or just watching TV. My mother was washing dishes with her back to me. When she turned back around in my direction, she was startled to find that I had gotten my hands on the bottle of cough syrup and had consumed every delicious drop.

At some point shortly after that, the cough syrup knocked me out. My parents called Dr. Vinson and then took me to his office. Dr. Vinson pumped my stomach. When I finally was coming to, I was screaming, "Help me, Daddy! Help me, Daddy, help me, help me!" Needless to say, I never drank cough medicine again after that. I suppose that was my first taste of taking life's bitter with the sweet. It would be far from my last time.

Not long after that, we moved away from the trailer on Maple Street to a regular house on Main Street. Because my parents were just renting at that time, they had more "freedom" to move. I guess that's one of the "freedoms" of not having very much money.

Mother was on the telephone one day and supposedly I was in the bathtub. At least that's what Mother thought, because she had put me in there. While she was on the phone, I saw a way I could get out and do something I had been really wanting to do, which was sit on the outside banister at the front of our house. Now, on the other side of this banister was about a twelve-foot drop to a concrete landing. Of course, that kind of danger isn't something that a three-year-old calculates. My entire mind was focused on climbing up on that banister, just because it was there.

I somehow reached the top of the banister and was perched there—naked as a jaybird. When you're a little kid, of course, you don't think anything about being buck naked. So there I was on my perch, enjoying nature and the view, when suddenly I spotted Daddy's police car coming over the hill toward the house. I thought, "Oh, no, I'm in trouble. I'm really going to catch it."

Before my little mind had time to think about what to do, Daddy very softly pulled in the driveway. He got out of the car and said, "Hey there, Dwana. Whatcha doin'?"

And I thought, "Well, maybe I'm not in trouble after all."

Daddy said in a very comforting way, "Hon, be careful. Don't you fall. Sit still. Sit still." The entire time he was steadily walking toward me. Before I knew it, he had reached out with those big arms of his, scooped me around the stomach, pulled me off the banister, and taken me into the house.

His tone then became less comforting. "What were you doing out there?! Where's your mother? You could have been killed!" Even a young birdbrain like me knew I was in trouble now. He proceeded to whip my butt good. I'm talking about a beating—brief, but hard. Keep in mind that I'm this little three-year-old gosling and I'm getting spanked—one, two, three, wham, wham, wham!—by this great big hand on my little bottom. It was the first time that he had ever spanked me, and it scared the daylights out of me.

Then, of course, he and Mother had words. She was horrified when she realized what had happened while she wasn't looking—and even worse, what could have happened. But that's not the end of the story.

The rest of the story is that we went on with life for about four or five days until somebody finally noticed that I wasn't going to the bathroom. And my tummy was hurting. So we once again got in the car and followed the familiar route to Dr. Vinson's office.

Dr. Vinson said, "Buford, she has had some kind of bad jarring. It's like she's kind of shut down. It's as if her intestines are asleep. Has anything happened? Has she had a fall? Has she been injured?"

Mother and Daddy both said no. Then Daddy remembered and said, "Well, the only thing I can think of that's happened is that I whipped her the other day because she was sitting up on a banister."

Dr. Vinson asked, "What did you whip her with and how did you whip her?"

Daddy said, "I just whipped her with my hand. I just took her and got her bottom and hit her about three licks."

Dr. Vinson shook his head and said, "Buford, do not ever, ever whip this child again. Let Pauline do it. Let your mother or whoever else do it, but you don't need to because you don't realize your own strength. With a child this small and your powerful hand, you have jarred her poor system. It's gone numb on us."

The good news was that I didn't get another whipping until I was thirteen. The bad news was that this first whipping was effective enough to last a full ten years. That an accidental overdose and a beating happen to be my first memories might give the wrong idea about my childhood, because there are plenty of memories that are a lot happier.

The tall sheriff of McNairy County. (Courtesy of *The Tennessean*)

There are also some that are much more terrifying and sad.

Not that I actually remember quite this far back, but I was born in Chicago on the night of January 9, 1961. I weighed nine pounds and ten ounces—four ounces more

Daddy and I play with his birddog in the front yard in the summer of 1962.

than my father had weighed when he was born twenty-three years earlier. I apparently was off to a hearty and healthy start. I was named Dwana Atoyia. To me, "Dwana" has kind of an Irish feel to it. I think my parents were inspired to name me that at least in part by a lady named Neewana, who lived in Daddy's hometown of Finger, Tennessee. Atoyia came from a TV show. My parents were trying to come up with a middle name for me while watching an episode of "Bonanza." There was a little Indian girl named Atoyia in that particular episode. My parents liked the sound of it and, maybe partly because my mother's mother was Cherokee, they thought it would be a good name for me.

Back in Adamsville in the first few months after I was born, my grandfather, Carl Pusser—we called him Papaw—who was chief of police, had been making plans. Because of an injury that was slowing him down and because he wanted his son back nearby, Papaw worked things out so that Daddy could take over his position. So that's how our family came to live in the lovely town of Adamsville in McNairy County, Tennessee.

I wasn't old enough to know one way or the other, but I'm sure now that my daddy was glad to be back home. I think the area is some of the most beautiful country anywhere. You've got the beautiful green grasslands and forests, you've got hills, you've got straight-aways and waterways, and that's all within McNairy County. Maybe I was just trying to get a better view of that same beautiful scenery when I climbed up on that banister the first chance I got.

The town of Adamsville also has many of the charms typical of a small town in the South. As I grew up, I loved to explore the shops along Main Street. My favorite was Walker's Grocery Store. It was the main "happening place" in town. Next door was a dime store called J&H Variety. Next door on the other side was Vinson's Drug Store, which Dr. Vinson's family owned. It also had a soda fountain,

which naturally was popular with the kids in town. They served milkshakes and ice cream.

I can still picture the layout of Walker's in my mind—just exactly how it was. I remember coming in with my daddy and going to the back of the store, where they served fresh country meats. You'd tell them how thick you wanted your baloney or ham cut for your sandwich, and Mr. Ed Luna, the butcher, would cut it to order. In the back where he was, it really was a Southern-style delicatessen. We'd shop for groceries every day. I always looked forward to the trip.

Before Walker's moved to that location, it was right next door to another grocery store called Seaton's. My parents shopped there a lot, too. We kids just loved it. It was much smaller than Walker's. Folks would walk in one store, get something, and then walk in the other store and get something else—charging purchases at both places and then paying at the end of the month.

Another downtown favorite for kids and adults was Slim's, the local hamburger joint. It was just a narrow storefront, only about twelve feet wide. Maybe that's why they called it Slim's. It could have been left open as an alley between buildings, but having Slim's there was a much more fun use of the space. At busy times, downtown could be filled with the aroma from Slim's as folks filed in for the house specialty, slug burgers, which are cereal burgers that taste far better than they sound.

The other downtown store that our family really liked was Winningham's Furniture. My daddy loved to go over there and talk to Mrs. Lucille Winningham. It was fun to browse around the store and dream about this or that piece of furniture that we might be able to have someday. Sometimes our dreams came true.

Our town was a perfect little town of the 1960s. You had your little general store, a clothing store, an appliance store (Jerry's TV repair shop, still there today), the thriving Audrey's Beauty Shop, a hardware store, and your gas stations—all right downtown. Adamsville was just a quiet, rural, Southern town. There were quaint, beautiful churches, and,

Dwana says:
Buford Pusser is his name and to be the Sheriff is his aim.

Dwana has worked real hard helping her Daddy campaign for Sheriff and asks everyone to please vote for him on August 6.

Don't forget to
Vote Buford Pusser For Sheriff Pd. Pol. Ad.

This newspaper ad shows me campaigning for Daddy when he ran for sheriff of McNairy County in 1964.

naturally, most everybody went to church on Sunday.

Of course, having Daddy as police chief added another dimension to my young perspective on life. Then in 1964, at the age of twenty-six, he became the youngest sheriff ever elected in Tennessee. I believe he still holds the record for that to this day. Being sheriff of the entire county, which covers over five hundred square miles, thrust a huge responsibility upon Daddy. It was a job he took very seriously. He'd burn up two tanks of gas a night as he patrolled the county looking for the thieves, gamblers, moonshiners, bootleggers, and all the other criminals who since the depression era had been making a mile-long stretch of Highway 45 at the state line one of the most corrupt and dangerous places in the South.

What was already bad became even worse during the 1950s when lawmen in Phenix City, Alabama, another Southern den of iniquity, had finally clamped down on the hardened criminals in their area. The nasty vipers that the police weren't able to nab slithered over to the Mississippi-Tennessee state line and set up their operations on that notorious stretch of

Highway 45 that was lined with seedy motels and brothels and illegal gambling houses and raucous taverns. And those were just the signs of badness you could easily see from the highway. It was the backrooms and the other parts of the underbelly of the area—the places that rarely saw the light of day—that were the most dangerous and despicable. The area soon earned the nicknames "Little Chicago" and "Murder City U.S.A." When the worst of the bad people needed to escape the heat of law enforcement in their own towns, they simply headed to this hoodlum haven.

Around the nation during this time, people were enjoying tuning in each week to "The Andy Griffith Show," television's version of a sheriff's family in a small, Southern town. Well, forget watching it on television once a week. In many ways, this little redheaded child was actually living that life every day.

Growing up, I loved watching this show because it was so similar to my life with a father who was the sheriff dealing with all of the characters around town. The difference, of course, was that Daddy was facing a much more dangerous element than Sheriff Andy Taylor ever encountered.

Around Mayberry, you might have to go somewhere like Mount Pilot to get into any real trouble. In McNairy County, you just had to go down to the state line, which was also the county line.

Daddy did indeed deal with some extremely tough, bad people and some very dangerous situations. I'll soon be getting to some of the stories that make that fact all too clear and illustrate how he was more than equal to the task. Any busting up he did was generally because something or somebody needed busting up. But in order to convey just how and why he was so well suited to the job of taking on the criminal and evil elements in the county, I first need to reveal more about his tender side.

Daddy was a big man. He was six foot six and 250 pounds. It took thirty-six-inch pant legs, a thirty-six-inch waist, and a size fifty-four extra-long jacket to fit him. Now, if you stop

There appeared to be scarcely an ounce of fat on Daddy when he was in shape. He sips a soft drink after we enjoyed a day on the water with a pontoon boat at Pickwick Landing State Park.

to think about it, a thirty-six-inch waist on a man of Daddy's height and weight is not very big. Where then was all that weight? The answer was behind the size fifty-four jacket. He had massive strength in his upper body and arms. Big or not, he always liked to be a sharp dresser. He was a gentle and dapper giant.

Most people don't think about Buford Pusser, the rough and tough sheriff who was out there fighting the criminal element, coming home every day and having also to be a father and eventually a mother to his young daughter and older stepdaughter and stepson. Daddy would help me with my homework. And it wasn't all work. He would take my friends and me to go and do special things, the same as other dads try to do for their kids whenever they can.

I remember one time when I was about eight, he took us up to Jackson, which is about an hour's drive northwest of Adamsville and is the nearest Tennessee city of a pretty good size. We went to see the premiere of *The Love Bug*. He got a bunch of my friends together, and we all rode in the squad car to Jackson. A real "Herbie" Love Bug car was there and everything. Afterward he treated us to pizza at the Pizza Inn, which was a really big deal for all of us kids because Adamsville didn't have a pizza place at that time.

On another occasion, people from "The Sheriff Big Jim

Show," a kiddie TV show in Jackson, called the jailhouse and reached my granddaddy.

Papaw told Daddy, "Buford, they've called from over at WBBJ and said you're supposed to bring Dwana and a group of her friends up to be on Sheriff Big Jim's show."

Oh, how I wanted to go! Not only was it a fun trip to a TV show, but they also gave you free McDonald's hamburgers. So, in the middle of all there was to do with his normal work, Daddy once again loaded up us kids in the car and took us to Jackson. We had a terrific time being on TV and then ate hamburgers at that famous place that always advertised on TV. This was really life in the fast lane for a little kid.

Of course, most of the fun times were just around Adamsville and our house. Daddy was a good cook. I can see him now wearing an apron, Bermuda shorts, sneakers, and a chef's hat and standing over the outdoor grill as he cooked hamburgers for all the kids in the neighborhood. He truly reveled in providing a wholesome, down-home time for friends and family. He was no master chef, but he loved flipping burgers and cooking a hot pot of chili.

I don't believe that Daddy ever grilled snake, but there was at least one day he could have. He was out taking target practice at bean cans, and I was setting up the cans so that he could shoot again. All of a sudden, Daddy firmly commanded, "Dwana, don't move." And of course I didn't. The next thing I knew—*blam*—he had fired a shot right next to me and taken the head off a snake that was coiled up beside me. I guess he was more comfortable with his shooting ability than he was with that snake rearing up to strike me.

I can also remember on Saturday afternoons, if Daddy were home, he would get out in the vacant lot on one side of our house, where the neighborhood boys would play baseball. There were a half a dozen or so boys within a year or two of each other in age around the neighborhood. Daddy would take batting practice with them. Of course, he could knock it to smithereens when he took a turn at bat. Given his druthers,

Daddy often played baseball with boys in the neighborhood. Here he is at the park with (left to right) Sam Robinson, Scotty Little, and Dale Bearden. (Courtesy of *The Tennessean*)

that was the kind of swinging of a big stick he preferred—just a nice game of baseball with the neighborhood kids.

On the other hand, if the call came in, he would go out that same night and bust up whiskey stills or put his life on the line by going in and taking care of whatever situation had to be handled. Especially when it came to the State Line Mob, he went full throttle and no holds barred.

He would tell stories about all the louts and lowlife thugs at the state line. When I asked him whether he was ever scared going in to deal with those people, he said, "Sure, there are times I'm scared, but I figure the people I'm going after are scared, too, and maybe with even more reason. The best thing I can do is to go in and hit the situation head on."

Yet even when he was fighting crime head on, Daddy

knew when a softer touch was needed. It was just his natural wisdom. It was also part of his personality to try to help people—especially kids who needed a little direction more than the full force of the law.

One particular time, he helped guide three teenagers after they stole his police car as a prank. They had ended up wrecking it, but not too badly. When Daddy caught up with the boys, he could have really come down hard on them. They would have had a juvenile record for car theft and a slew of other offenses. It could have been really bad for them and embarrassing for their families. It could have ruined the boys' futures. What Daddy did instead was take a switch—just a normal-sized switch, not a big stick or anything like that—and pretty much just wear them out by switching them on their legs.

Perhaps recalling Dr. Vinson's warning about not knowing his own strength, Daddy was mindful not to use overpowering force. All he was trying to do was make an instructive point with the boys. There can be little doubt that the boys nevertheless felt every bit of the "instruction" that Daddy intended and that they also knew this was their one and only warning. They knew he was capable of finding bigger switches but that he deliberately hadn't this time. Daddy then took the boys home to their parents, who more than likely found their own sizes of switches for their sons.

All of this is not to say that the Pusser household was immune to petty crimes by a child of its own. And so I must confess to mine.

When Daddy became sheriff, my mother went to work as the cook for the jail. It was in the courthouse at Selmer, the county seat and a lovely little town, about twelve miles from Adamsville. Mother would cook meals for my daddy and his staff and for the prisoners. She did most of her shopping for the jailhouse right there in Selmer. One of her favorite places to shop was a little grocery store called Jernigan's, where the sheriff's office had a charge account. This was the first time I knew about the wonderful notion of charging for something now and paying later. I caught on to the idea of how charging was supposed to work while watching my mother shop many times at Jernigan's.

During that time, a big, fancy store opened in Selmer and we went to check it out. It was a humdinger of a store, the likes of which I had never seen before. I was thrilled by this new shopping experience. We were getting groceries one day, and at the end of one of the aisles there was a display rack that spun around. It was filled with all varieties of garden seeds, including ones for watermelons.

I knew that my granddaddy grew watermelons. I told my mother, "I want to get these watermelon seeds for Papaw."

I enjoy a big slice of watermelon with my grandfather and Daddy.

"No, you're not getting those seeds for him," Mother replied. "He's got his own seeds. Besides, that's probably not the kind he uses."

Well, I wanted those seeds terribly badly, so as Mother went on with her shopping, I went back and I got them. I rejoined my mother. As we were checking out, when my mother wasn't looking, I looked at the little sack boy and said, "Here, add this to our ticket." I folded the packet of seeds up, ran out, got in our car, and waited for my mother.

We got to the courthouse and rode the elevator up to the fourth floor, which is where the jail was. I knew I'd find my granddaddy there because he helped Daddy out as jailor. I ran in there and said, "Papaw, Papaw, look what I got you! I got you some watermelon seeds!"

I knew he'd be so proud that I'd brought him a present. I loved Papaw dearly. Instead, he asked my mother, "Pauline, why in this world did you let her get these seeds?"

"I didn't let her get them," Mother responded.

"Well, somebody let her get them. Dwana, did you steal those?"

"No, Papaw, I told the sack boy to add it on to the ticket."

"Well, you stole them if your mother told you not to get them."

One of the policemen drove me back down to the big, fancy store—pronto. He marched me in there and I had to confess to my sin of stealing the watermelon seeds. But after I told them that I had taken them, I pointed out quickly that I had told the sack boy to put them down on our ticket. Like a true fink, I was looking to put the blame on somebody else. But of course, he was the sack boy, not the cashier, so he couldn't possibly have tried to put them on our ticket as I had told him. That was the first and the last time I ever stole anything in my life. I learned my lesson.

And if having my family and the local sheriff watch my every move wasn't bad enough, there was always Santa Claus to worry about, at least for a while. When I was five years old, my parents were having dinner out one night shortly before the Christmas that was to be my mother's last. My brother, Mike, told me to go look in the closet in our parents' bedroom, because I might find something interesting.

Even though their closet felt like someplace that ought to be off limits to me, I couldn't resist. When I opened the closet, I found a great big, beautiful doll and a racecar set. My brother and I played with them and then covered our tracks by putting them neatly back in the closet. When Christmas Day arrived and the doll and racecar set were under the tree from Santa, I was confused. I was thrilled to have the new doll but worried whether there really was a Santa. A few months later I asked my grandmother, Mamaw, "There's never been a Santa Claus, has there?"

"No, Dwana, there's no Santa Claus," she replied, just as matter-of-factly as if she were reading a grocery list.

Between that Christmas and the next, an older friend of mine got a little step-in, step-out motorbike, a primitive version of today's mopeds or scooters. I wanted one so badly. I was going to turn seven in January, and I begged for one for Christmas. Daddy snuck out and bought one, brought it to our house on Christmas Eve, and sat it on the front porch. When our dog, Old Bull, started barking, I asked, "Bull, why are you barking? What's wrong?"

I looked out the window to see what was the matter, and there on the porch was Daddy, trying to get the little motorbike up on its kickstand. I was really excited, but I stayed quiet about what I saw. When the bike arrived from Santa the next morning, I was delighted. I was perfectly happy having Daddy be my Santa.

Whether there was a real Santa Claus or not, if I ever got the feeling that I couldn't get away with anything because somebody was always watching me, I might have been right. Here's a case in point. I wanted to learn how to swim, which, of course, my daddy knew was a good thing to do even if I hadn't been so eager. He signed me up for lessons down at the public swimming pool with a man named Mr. Bill Webb.

Mr. Bill told me some years later, "You know, Dwana, your

daddy would bring you down there for those lessons. He was worried about you and he didn't know me that well at the time. I would see him standing back over at the other side of the pool building, where he could see exactly what I was doing in trying to help you swim."

During the time he was giving me lessons, Mr. Bill probably never knew about the threats that were made on our lives. I guess Daddy was a little leery of just about everybody.

Mr. Bill continued, "After about three days of your father standing over there watching while I gave you swimming lessons, he finally trusted me enough to where he felt comfortable leaving you."

It eventually became the routine that, when I was done with my lessons, I'd just call the jailhouse and they'd put out a call to whichever deputy was nearest to take me back home.

As a parent myself now, I think part of my daddy's staying and watching the lessons might have been just his wanting to be there to see his child learning something new. I know that can be a great joy for any parent.

Even though I had been keen on learning how to swim and loved the water, I have not always taken to everything on the water. When I was about twelve years old, Daddy bought a pontoon boat. He took us kids out on the boat quite often. I remember one particular day when we went out on the boat, Daddy was bound and determined to teach me to water-ski. He had a friend named Mike Bolton, who was really into boats and skiing. Mike was appointed my ski instructor. He got in the water with me and was providing his very best instruction, but I was just flailing away and having no luck getting up, failed attempt after failed attempt.

Daddy was driving the boat and kept on encouraging me, saying, "Dwana, you've got to get up." Finally, Mike said to me, "Dwana, I'm going to tell you something. If you don't get up this time, you and I both are going to get killed, because do you see that lightning that's striking down and headed this way? I know your daddy's stubborn enough and determined enough that he's gonna see you up on these skis today. So I suggest for the sake of your life and mine that you get up this time."

Guess what . . . I got up that time. It was thrilling. But I don't know who was happiest, me or Daddy—or Mike!

Those are some of the playful, or at least relatively harmless, memories that I have about growing up around Adamsville and Selmer. It is when you head south of Selmer on Highway 45, down around the state line and the area toward Corinth, Mississippi, that the memories become darker. Sometimes that darkness reached up and grabbed the gentler areas around Selmer and even Adamsville.

As a child, I was so scared of the areas where the bad people hung out that, whenever we went to Corinth, I would lie down on the floorboard of the car when we passed through the main part of the state line where the Shamrock Motel, the White Iris, the Plantation Club, and other notorious joints were located. I was grown up and driving before I finally realized there was another way to Corinth besides that main route on Highway 45. It took longer, but it was worth it to me because it was far less traumatic.

One day when I was a very young child, I was at the jail and I overheard my granddaddy talking to Daddy about threatening calls. Mother had received a couple of them, and Papaw received one at the jail. This man was threatening to kill my grandfather and all of us children unless Daddy stopped his crusade against crime down at the state line. The man said he was going to take us down to the Hatchie Bottom, which is a swamp area down by the Hatchie River, an offshoot of the Tennessee River. He went on to say that when he was done killing us, he was going to bring our bodies back to town and put them on display on the courthouse lawn.

It scared me to death when I overheard this. It was bad enough to fear every day for my daddy's life, but to have it compounded by fear for my own life was pretty hard for a little kid.

Daddy was not so naïve that he didn't have a healthy fear about dangerous situations, but when his family was threatened, you did not want to be anywhere along his warpath. He was pretty sure who was calling with the threats. He believed it was a bad guy named Carl ("Towhead") White. He was the boyfriend of Louise Hathcock, queen bee of the State Line Mob. I'll have more to say about her later.

Anyway, Daddy set out one day to round up Towhead White for making the threats. Towhead was raised in Sumner, Mississippi, and had a taste for $200 Italian suits, the kind that today would probably cost ten times that amount. It was the sort of outfit that you just didn't see regular folks wearing around McNairy County, then or now.

Daddy spotted White lurking around the notorious Shamrock Motel at dusk, just about the time White would likely begin his nightly no-goodness. Daddy told White to get in the car with him. Daddy and White then went for a little ride down the road. They ended up at the Hatchie Bottom.

Daddy made White get out of the car and crawl around in the swamp, handcuffed and begging for his life. This went on for most of the night. Then Daddy said to him, "I'm telling you, Towhead—I know you're behind this. If you call my wife or my daddy and threaten either of them or my children, I promise you I will be back to get you and we'll be back here—if I get one more phone call."

The phone calls stopped.

When things like the threatening phone calls happened, I'm sure it made my daddy think twice about having me hang around the courthouse. On the other hand, he probably figured that the courthouse was about as safe a place for me as anywhere, because there was always somebody there—Daddy or his deputies or Papaw. And my mother was also there a lot, cooking meals.

I basically was raised in the courthouse. I knew every nook and cranny in the building, and I knew everybody, too, whether crook or granny. I just loved it.

We had an old janitor there we called Mr. Joe. He was maybe five foot two and always wore overalls. He had to put up with me a lot because we were both constantly rambling around the courthouse. He was working and I was messing around and getting into stuff, such as in Mr. Flake Smith's office. Underneath a certain counter in his office, Mr. Flake always kept a fifty-pound bag of peanuts. I was forever going in there and getting myself out a big handful or even a pocketful of snacks.

Everybody in the courthouse spoiled me. If I wanted something to drink, I'd go up to somebody and say all pitiful-like, "I sure am thirsty. I wish I had something to drink."

They'd respond, "Oh, here, honey," and give me a dime and maybe a nickel, too, so I could get a cold drink and a candy bar. There was also a little place across the street that sold ice cream.

Sometimes a drink or candy bar or even an ice cream wasn't enough to keep me occupied and out of trouble. One night we were up at the jail late, and Mr. D. A. Parrish, one of Daddy's friends with the Highway Patrol, came by and joined us for a supper that Mother had cooked. The four of us were sitting around the little yellow-topped, chrome-legged table that helped give sort of a homey feel to the area just outside the jail's kitchen. Against a wall on the way to the kitchen was a sink with a shelf above it where Daddy kept his hairbrush and toothpaste and that sort of thing.

D. A. Parrish was a great big, mostly bald-headed man, about as big as Daddy. In fact, a lot of people used to call each one by the other's name just to aggravate them. Anyway, Daddy had this new metal-handled hairbrush. He got it from the barbershop, so it was a substantial, heavy-duty brush. Well, I saw the brush. And there sat Mr. D. A. Parrish with his bald head.

Being a kid and ready for a little mischief, I picked up that brush and, when nobody was looking, I went up behind Mr. Parrish and crowned him with the brush really good. It was no surprise that the blow knocked him unconscious for a few seconds. The brush was so heavy—or Mr. Parrish's head was so hard—that the impact bent the back of the brush.

I didn't notice what shape Mr. Parrish's head was in right then, but I did instantly know that I was in big trouble. I tried to run, but before I could get gone, Daddy had reached out and grabbed me. There he was holding me with one hand and trying to lift D. A.'s unconscious head back up with the other. Needless to say, that was my last "brush" with that sort of mischief.

Not to make light of my attack on Mr. Parrish, but I was involved in situations at the courthouse that were a whole lot more serious. Even Mr. Parrish would have agreed they were.

One of the worst times was one Sunday morning in 1967 when my granddaddy and I were preparing breakfasts for the prisoners. He was making the meals and I was delivering them. One area of cells was where they kept the prisoners who were thought to be a higher risk, such as suspected killers and other violent offenders. They were kept in cells with virtually solid metal doors—the kind with a diamond-shaped peephole to see in and out of and then a sliding panel at the floor for passing a tray of food through.

I was making my rounds and stopped at this one cell. I slid the tray through the door and said, "Breakfast is here."

Nobody said anything. I said again, "Your breakfast is here," because the prisoners usually said, "O.K." or "Thank you" or at least grunted.

There was still no sound, so I bent down to look through the tray opening. When I slid the panel back and looked in and then up, I saw that the prisoner had hanged himself with a bedsheet. My innocent little eyes had to see it that Sunday morning.

That wasn't enough to keep me from wanting to spend time around the jail, but it did make me realize—in a very sobering way for anybody but especially for a six-year-old child—that the jail was not a place of fun and games. It was a lesson I would soon learn again in a different way. Here's what happened.

I was allowed to walk around the corridors where the cells were. I'd go back there and I guess do things that a kid might do that were aggravating to the prisoners.

Maybe I'd driven one of the prisoners to the breaking point with my antics. This one day, a jailbird decided he was going to escape. He had tried it once before by jumping off the fourth-story roof of the courthouse onto a nearby tree. Unfortunately, for him at least, he didn't hit the tree exactly where he thought he would, and—snap, crackle, pop—after hitting quite a few branches on his four-story way to the ground, he finally landed. It's a wonder the fall didn't kill him. I guess the branches broke his fall. But they also broke a leg or two and some ribs. After necessary medical treatment, he was back in his cell.

He had just gotten healed up good when I came along playing in the corridor. He decided to try another escape. This time his flight wouldn't be solo or airborne. Instead, he decided to take someone as his hostage—me.

I was standing there at the bars to his cell and talking. He said, "Dwana, turn around and back up here. I want to see how tall you've gotten. Let me measure you."

I turned around and backed up to the bars, and when I did, he put his arm around me. He had kept a knife—I guess from one of the trays or else he had made it—and he pointed it near my neck. I immediately started screaming, "Papaw! Papaw!"

And the man was hollering, "Mr. Pusser! Mr. Pusser!"

My granddaddy came down the corridor as fast as he could, but he was still pretty crippled from an accidental fall and was using a walking stick.

The man said, "You're gonna let me out or I'm gonna stab her."

Papaw was of course trying to settle the man down and talk him out of it. I was frantically screaming and carrying on and kicking and I'm sure giving the man his money's worth. I could feel the knifepoint as the prisoner poked it at my shoulder while he was yelling at my granddaddy to let him out.

This went on for a bit, and then I heard the elevator go "ding." I thought, "Oh boy, maybe we've got help." The ding must have caught the attention of the man, too, because his grip on me loosened just a little.

In a split second, I realized that I had a chance. I bit the man's arm as hard as I could and he reflexively let go. I took off yelling and running as fast as I could. I'm sure the man was in pain, but I didn't stop to check.

As I was running the zigzag path out of the cell area, whom did I run into stepping out of the elevator but Daddy. I was screaming, and he was trying to figure out what I was saying.

"Where's Papaw?" he asked.

Out of breath and scared, I just pointed. He rushed back to the cell area. I don't know exactly what transpired back there, but when they came out, granddaddy's walking stick was broken. I think it's safe to say that they beat the living daylights out of the man.

I was seven years old at the time, but my days of being allowed back in the cell area like Opie Taylor of Mayberry were over.

CHAPTER 2

Daddy's Childhood

I think it would be a good idea for me to tell a little about my family roots and history. My father's father, Carl Pusser (Papaw to me), worked on the pipeline in Louisiana, Texas, Oklahoma, and Ohio. Before he did pipeline work, he was a sharecropper and an independent farmer. He grew peanuts, cotton, and corn. He also worked in a sawmill for about fifty cents a day. I've heard that he did a little haircutting, so I suppose he was a barber as well.

He was a big, heavyset man and tough, like most of the Pussers. How tough? I remember one time I had fed one of our cats part of a can of cat food and put the rest of the can in the refrigerator to give to the cat later on. Papaw couldn't see very well or maybe just didn't notice the label, but he thought the cat food was a can of potted meat. He got the can out of the refrigerator and made himself a nice sandwich for a snack. He apparently enjoyed the sandwich, because he never said anything until the next day when I looked in the refrigerator and asked him if he had seen my can of cat food. "What cat food? I haven't seen any cat food," he barked. When I described the can that had been in the refrigerator, he about had a cow.

Speaking of which, one time Papaw gave two giant pills intended for sick cows to two of our dogs when they seemed to be as sick as some of our cows had been. The only problem was that Papaw gave them the full cow dose instead of splitting the pills in half. That might not have been the only

42

problem with giving those pills to the dogs. In any case, both dogs died. No doubt the dogs would have been better off eating cans of that "potted meat" instead.

The first Pussers to come to the United States were actually "Pursers," who settled in North Carolina by way of Jamestown, Virginia, after sailing to America from England around 1635. Papaw's grandfather, Richard Pusser, settled in Finger, Tennessee, in 1879. He had come to Tennessee from Georgia, where his father, John Pusser, was too old to hit the battle trail when the Civil War erupted, but John served in the home militia in Pulaski County. While old John may or may not have skirmished with General Sherman's troops as they marched through Georgia, his brother, Solomon Pusser, did fight in the War Between the States and died in a Yankee prison in Maryland.

My father's mother, Helen Harris Pusser (Mamaw to me), was a survivor and one tough lady. She was born in 1908 near Finger. Most of the big bones and height of our family seem to come from my grandmother's side of the family, the Harrises. Her brother was principal of the school in Finger. I think my daddy's mannerisms and personality were more like the Harrises.

Papaw was farming and living with his father in Chester County when he met my grandmother at an all-day singing at a Methodist church. They married on August 5, 1928. They had three children: John Howard, the oldest; sister Gailya; and Buford Hayse, who was the youngest. They were all four years apart. Daddy was born in 1937 near Leapwood, but their mailing address was Finger.

They lived in the Jim Moore Place, about a mile west of Leapwood on the Leapwood-Finger Road. The house had four rooms, a fireplace, and a big, long front porch. It was built high off the ground.

The family lived a typical country lifestyle of the depression era. They did what they had to in order to get by. They had a garden, and my grandmother would milk the cows, gather the eggs from the hens' nests, and make breakfast

Mamaw holds me in late winter of 1961, just before I notch my first birthday.

over an old wood cook stove. Then she'd walk to catch the bus to the textile factory, where she worked a full day.

My daddy was born on a cold day. Papaw had to go three or four miles to call Dr. Tucker. Daddy was born about one o'clock in the morning—just before the doctor got there. Miss Daisy Garner was the one who actually delivered him, just as the doctor came in the door.

It was obvious that Daddy inherited the family trait of lots of hair. He had his first bowl haircut before his first birthday. I bet Papaw cut it.

Daddy was a pretty good-sized baby. He seemed to enjoy older people. Mamaw said that he was always quiet as a boy and that he liked to be by himself. When it came time for him to start school, Daddy wanted no part of it. He wanted to stay home with my grandmother. Yes, I'll say it: Buford Pusser was a mama's boy!

Daddy didn't want to leave home on that first day of school. He said that he wanted to wait until he was forty, but Mamaw said he could wait only until his birthday in December, when he would turn six. Despite Daddy's reluctance to start school, Mamaw said that he was always a leader. The other kids just seemed naturally to follow him.

When he first went to Leapwood School, bullies picked

Daddy was just one year old when this photo was taken near his birthplace in Finger, Tennessee, on December 30, 1938.

on him. Perhaps that is one of the ways he learned to sympathize with the underdog.

As a boy, he played with a slingshot, had pet chickens, and played a lot with his sister, Gailya. Because Daddy had such beautiful dark hair, Gailya would sometimes dress him up in a dress and high-heel shoes. Being a good younger brother, he put up with that to a certain extent, but he didn't want anybody to see him. He almost always played with girls during his early childhood, simply because there happened to be a lot more of them around his immediate neighborhood. It seemed that throughout his life, girls were drawn to my father. He liked them, too.

The family had a birddog that Daddy would take with him when he went fishing. One time when he was about eight years old, Daddy and his brother and sister went to look for a whippoorwill's nest. While they were looking for the nest, they came upon the body of a neighbor girl who was Daddy's age. She had drowned in a ditch after a hard

Daddy and his brother, John, left, and sister, Gailya, were typical depression-era farm kids in the community of Finger, Tennessee. When Daddy entered the eighth grade, he and his parents moved to Adamsville.

rain. The floodwaters carried her to a corn patch on the Pusser farm. Daddy was very upset after seeing the body, which the adults brought to the house and cleaned up.

By the time Daddy got to be a big boy, he was seeing the fun of playing practical jokes. I remember hearing about one he played on his granddaddy, Bliss Harris, who had come to stay with the family. They had an outhouse, and my great-grandfather Harris went outside to use it. Daddy knew he was in there. He fired a shotgun and rained a storm of pellets against the side of the outhouse. When his grandpa came running out with his pants hanging down below his knees, Daddy thought it was the funniest thing he had ever seen.

One boyhood pal recalls attending Decoration Day at the Mars Hill church when Daddy was around twelve years old. The church had no bathrooms or even an outhouse, so folks went to the bushes when the call of nature came. Men went one way and the women another. Daddy and his friend came across two little boys who were fighting, and one of the youths had just pulled a pocketknife from his pocket. Daddy calmly approached the kid and took it away from him, but not before the boy cut Daddy on the wrist.

Daddy's friend ran and told Papaw what had happened. Papaw told the boy, "Why, son, he'll be all right." Sure enough, when he came back, Daddy had simply tied a handkerchief around his wrist and acted as though nothing had happened.

The family moved to Adamsville in 1951 when Daddy was in the eighth grade. Mamaw said that Daddy "just barely got by," referring to his scholastics, but the teachers said he could make friends easily.

Mamaw had gone to work in Henderson at the shirt factory for a year when Daddy was five. In 1947, she worked at a factory in Adamsville making slips. Later it became a shirt factory, and in 1956 it became unionized.

When Mamaw was considering moving to Adamsville, Papaw didn't want to move. The next time Papaw came back from working on the pipeline, he found that Mamaw had moved the family to Adamsville and into a house on Baptist Street. Mamaw got things done, and she did it her way.

Schoolboy Buford Pusser, at age eleven.

Long before Clint Eastwood's Dirty Harry was cool in sunglasses in San Francisco, Daddy wore shades in Finger, Tennessee.

Mamaw also knew how to use a gun. Late one night shortly after she had moved the family to Adamsville, she heard a rapping at the door and thought somebody was trying to break in. Being new to city life (Adamsville had a population of about a thousand people, which seemed like a lot to a family from Leapwood), she didn't know what city folks might do. She hollered for whomever it was to go away. And she warned him that she had a gun, and if he kept trying to get in, she was ready to shoot. The noise started up once again, and sure enough, Mamaw fired her shotgun through the door and went back to bed. The rest of the night was silent. The next morning she got up and found the family cat stone-cold dead on the front porch.

Now off the farm and becoming a town boy, Daddy got his first job around age twelve at Duren's, the general store. He sacked and delivered groceries and ran all sorts of errands. One of his favorite treats there was milk. He gulped it down by the pint and said it made his arms grow strong. He always was big for his age.

Daddy was always a sharp dresser. At a time when most of the kids wore blue jeans and T-shirts—not unlike today— Daddy wore starched khakis. I think he had only two pairs, so Mamaw was washing and ironing a pair every day.

One of Daddy's boyhood pals and a close friend for all of his life was Roger Horton, who also was raised in the Leapwood community. Roger was two years older than Daddy. They were just like brothers.

"Buford was pretty good-sized boy, kind of shy," Roger remembers. "We were normal kids. We liked wrestling and scuffling in school. Helen kept him pretty well under control. I went over to his house and stayed all night a lot of times. His daddy was gone a lot working on the pipeline.

"They had an old car. When Helen was with him, he'd be puttering along in an old Hudson, but when she'd send him to the store by himself, he'd have it speeded up and it would be smoking 'cause it needed rings," Roger says.

He adds, "Coach Max Hile was Adamsville's first football

coach. He had played some football at Notre Dame. I think the first Adamsville High football team was in 1950 or 1951.

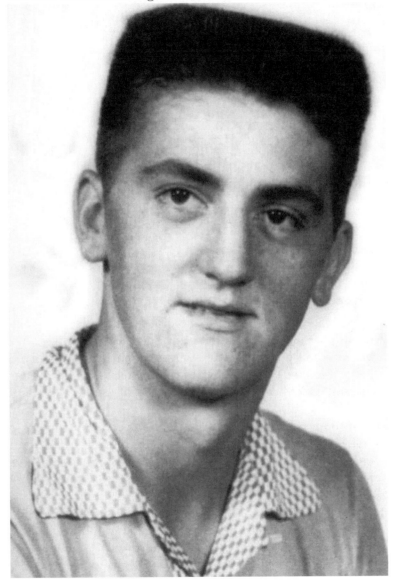

Daddy wears a crew cut at age sixteen.

Daddy, who always wore those khaki pants, worked at Duren's Supply Company when he was in high school. Pictured here (from left) are: Mac Fondren, Charles H. Duren, Mrs. Duren, Mr. Duren, and Daddy.

Coach Hile later became principal. I remember one day when Buford and I and another friend played hooky. We were hanging around at Walter Snodgrass's poolroom, and Coach Hile came looking for us. The poolroom had a front door and a side door. Max thought he had us as he came in through the side door, but we went out the front. The only one of us he recognized was Buford. Buford and I and the other boy ran off a little way and hid under the floor of a service station, where we could look out onto the street. We laid under there three or four hours until all the other kids got out of school."

Roger finishes with more memories of Daddy's driving. "Buford worked at Duren's. I remember he drove a flatbed International truck and delivered groceries. He was always driving fast. I'd ride with him a lot of times when he came to Leapwood. It was a gravel road and he'd have that old flatbed slinging around the curves. Later, when he was

Daddy had a lean and hungry look during his high-school years and loved to drink milk. He believed that the beverage made him stronger.

sheriff, I rode with him at 135 miles per hour. That was just the way he drove."

It's obvious that Daddy was not exactly devoted to studying

Daddy was slim and trim as a high-school student in 1954.

during his high-school years—a fact that is readily borne out by his report cards, which are in the Buford Pusser Museum, our old house in Adamsville. I suspect he was allergic to homework. Had it not been for school sports, I don't know if Daddy would have made it to graduation day.

He once got into hot water in Miss Cora Hair's class. She was a little bitty lady, about five feet tall with white hair. If you misbehaved, she would whack you over the head with a history book while she bit into a pencil.

She often told her classes this story: "I can say something that few other people can say. I whipped Buford Pusser. I came into my classroom one day and found two holes about the size of your head in the top of my desk. Buford was standing on top of my brand-new desk wrestling with four or five other boys. As they tugged and pulled on him, Buford's weight sent him sinking knee-deep through my desk. After the dust settled, I brought him around to the front of my desk and tore him up with my paddle."

Daddy was a good football player for the hometown Adamsville Cardinals. Even so, he hated all of the hollering during practice and games. His football and basketball coach was T. E. Chisholm.

I am told that when Daddy was a freshman trying out for the basketball team, he was big but not quick. Instead of running Daddy up and down the basketball court, Coach Chisholm tried to make a boxer out of him. He put gloves on Daddy and had him spend lots of time pummeling a boxing bag.

Daddy didn't especially enjoy football, as he played fullback on offense and tackle near the middle of the line on defense. Most unpleasant were the preseason practices in August. One particular day, it was even more brutally hot than usual. At the end of an exhausting practice, the coach still made the team run laps around the field in the blazing afternoon sun. It was torture for all the players, but it was perhaps especially so for Daddy, who had to endure it all with asthma.

After practice, Daddy went home and told Mamaw about

Daddy, number 23 (top right), played fullback and tackle for the Adamsville High School Cardinals. The coaches were T. E. Chisholm, right, and Max Hile, left.

how much he and the other players had suffered in the heat and yet still had to run laps. Mamaw gave him some advice about how to deal with the situation. The next day, the coach again made the squad run around the football field five times as a disciplinary measure. Following Mamaw's advice, Daddy got all the boys to fall out on the ground on his cue, as if they had all passed out because of heat exhaustion. The boys thought it was hilarious, but the coach didn't laugh. That stunt no doubt just earned them more laps around the field.

Don Browder was a good friend of my daddy's during their school years. He remembers, "We would take turns spending the night at each other's house, and we played a lot of sports together. Buford was a shy kid, not loud or obnoxious, but very quiet and an average student who struggled with his studies. He did dress nicely. You would have thought him the most unlikely of heroes."

He continues, "We were one-on-one partners in football practice because we were the two biggest players on the team. One day we were having one-on-one tackle drills, which we were supposed to run through at full speed, and I hit him and it liked to knock me out. After the collision, we were both lying on the ground. Buford started to get up, and I said, 'For god's sake, Pusser, lie down. You're gonna kill me.'

He was six foot five inches tall and weighed about 220 pounds then. If they would've had body building like they do today, he would have been awesome. He was naturally muscular."

Don Browder recalls that Daddy was president of the A Club (Athletic Club) and voted best all-around and best athlete during their senior year at Adamsville High School.

Daddy played ball because the coaches asked him to, but Mamaw always said that he didn't really enjoy it. She said that he would rather have been by himself. Nevertheless, I have to believe that once his natural talent started coming through, he enjoyed the sports, because that was the only area in which he excelled during his school years. Sports also gave him an outlet for cutting up, which was perhaps his favorite sport of all.

Childhood friend Paul Wallace Plunk tells a story about Daddy. Around Halloween one time when they were teenagers, a bunch of the boys visited a man's barn and "borrowed" his wagon. They took it over to the nearby town of Crump and dismantled it. Then, piece by piece, they put it back together on top of the porch over Crump Mercantile Store.

The next morning, there was the wagon catching the sun's first rays high above the store. Nobody knew how the wagon got up there. The boys had to go across one building, which was low in the back, to climb on top of the store. The owner eventually figured out how the prank was accomplished and declared that nobody would be using his building for access again to take the wagon down. A couple of nights later, back the pranksters went and, using their same methods, left the reassembled wagon at the store owner's back door, just to make the point that they could do whatever they wanted to do.

Paul Wallace also remembers how Daddy and some of his friends would sneak away from school on occasion. The boys would hide out on top of a water tower or get on top of the buildings downtown when the principal would come looking for them.

Failing in two subjects in March of his junior year, Daddy

Daddy, right, and a couple of pals had a big time in high school when they went to the Mid-South Fair in Memphis in the mid-1950s.

asked his mother if he could go to Oklahoma to work on the pipeline where his father was working at that time. He promised Mamaw that he would come back and graduate. He went to Wynnewood, Oklahoma, where he worked for about two months. He kept his word and came back to school the next fall. His mother worked with him to get him caught up in his studies.

Billy Frank Harris, Daddy's younger cousin by three years, remembers that on Decoration Day 1955, at Maggie Jones Methodist Church, his daddy had recently bought a new Chevrolet. His older brother, Bobby, raced it against Daddy and some other boys in a 1954 Ford on a blacktop road in Leapwood. By the time they got back to the churchyard, Billy Frank and Bobby's daddy had already found out they had been racing. He gave them all a whipping.

Paul Wallace Plunk recalls another tale. "Our bunch was feuding with a group from Savannah [Tennessee]. Their leader was a fellow they called Big Red Hubbard, who was not as tall as Buford but was really stocky and solid. The two groups always wanted Buford and Big Red to fight, but they never would—probably because each respected the other.

"Buford was hanging out near the high school with his group of friends one time when he decided to leave and walk down the street alone toward the high school. Nobody thought anything about it, and the rest of the fellas just stayed hanging around. A carload of the other group drove down the same street that Buford had gone down. Not long after that, Buford came back to his pals and said, 'Those sorry S.O.B.s cut me.'"

Paul Wallace continues, "Buford showed everybody the cut on his leg. Everybody believed him, but what had really happened was that he had gone to cut down the volleyball net at the school, and his knife slipped and he had cut his own leg. But he didn't let on to his buddies about that. Instead, he used it as the foundation for some future mischief.

"A few days later, Buford told his mother that I wanted to borrow his daddy's shotgun to go squirrel hunting. Those 'squirrels' just happened to live in Savannah and liked to play pool and drive fast.

"Buford spotted the car of Savannah squirrels and let go with nine shots into the back of that car. It was like a Wild West show. We then drove off down a little road and hid next

Daddy sat front and center grasping the ball when this photograph was
made of his high-school basketball team. The coach was T. E. Chisholm.

to the river bottom near the levee. We were sure that any
minute we'd hear police sirens. But nothing happened and
nothing was ever said."

During Daddy's senior year, he became a basketball star.
He averaged nearly twenty points a game and about that
many rebounds as well. That year the team went to the
regionals, but Daddy wasn't able to play in the regional
finals because he caught the mumps. The team still quali-
fied for the final sixteen, but with Daddy at home, sick and
with swollen cheeks, the team lost. Before graduating in
1956, he lettered several times in football and basketball. I
really do believe it was athletics that enabled him to stay in
school. As soon as he graduated, Daddy was ready for
adventures that didn't involve a classroom.

CHAPTER 3

Daddy's Early Adulthood

As big and strong as he was, Daddy was offered a football scholarship to play at Florida State University, but he had had his fill of organized sports. What he really wanted to be was a United States Marine. He made up his mind to follow that dream.

He worked at Duren's store that summer after high school, and then, on August 9, 1956, he hopped a bus to Jackson and then Nashville. There he caught a train that took him to basic training at Parris Island, South Carolina.

Daddy was a crack shot with a rifle, but unfortunately his dream of a career in the military was not to hit its mark. He was a Marine for three short months. He had tried to get himself stationed somewhere up north because he knew his asthma symptoms would have been less obvious, but the Marines weren't about to cater to the wishes of a new recruit. And so it was that six of his twelve weeks as a Marine were served in the military hospital because of his asthma.

Honorably discharged on November 14, Daddy proudly wore that Marine uniform for the last time as he made his way home. The rule was that a discharged soldier could wear his uniform until sundown on the day he came home. Daddy waited until the last glimmer of sunlight to take off his uniform. He was that proud of being a Marine. He came home with $100 in his pocket, courtesy of the Marines, but the pride he felt from having served in the Corps, even for a short time, was priceless.

Pvt. Buford Pusser, U.S.M.C.

Freshly back in civilian life, Daddy was riding back from Memphis with his friend Billy Earl Christopher on November 25, 1956, when their car crashed and Daddy made a fast,

Just a two weeks out of the Marines, Daddy was seriously injured in a November 1956 car accident. His face was still bandaged when he returned from the hospital in January.

unintentional exit through the windshield. That resulted in three crushed vertebrae in his back and forty days of recuperation in Baptist Hospital in Memphis. He was released on January 4, 1957.

Daddy had to wear a brace for eight weeks. He then went to work for Shackleford Funeral Home in Selmer, from March to September 1957.

There were certain aspects to this job that he loved. First, he got to drive the Cadillac ambulance. Talk about sitting in high cotton. He also got to do some embalming and other tasks to help prepare the deceased. After dressing one of his first bodies, he called his mother and said, "I know you don't know this person, but I want you to come by and see how he looks." It was a strange request, perhaps, but Daddy always took pride in his work.

While in high school, Daddy had taken several jaunts with his buddies down to the honky-tonks around the notorious state line area. They went mostly just to stand around and gawk, as schoolboys do. However, a trip in March 1957 marked his first physical encounter with the State Line

Mob. Daddy had about three hundred dollars on him when he decided to take an adventurous peek inside the Plantation Club. He was thirsty and also wanted to try his hand at a few games of chance.

He started winning but then caught one of the housemen changing the dice on him during a game of craps. After making an accusation, Daddy got jumped by four of the workers. They proceeded to pistol-whip him and stomp him in the head and face once he was on the floor. After robbing him of all his money, they pitched him out into the cold rain to die.

Daddy didn't die. He somehow got himself up and drove to the clinic in Selmer, where he wound up having 192 stitches sewed into his head and chest. He would neither forgive nor forget those who were responsible for the beating he received.

Disappointed at the low wages he was making at the funeral home, Daddy quit and spent three or four weeks working out of state on a pipeline job with Papaw.

Fate was not kind to Papaw around this time. After working on the pipeline and at the shirt factory, he decided to accept the job as police chief of Adamsville. Then he was injured in a truck wreck in October 1957. The injury required hip surgery. Papaw spent five weeks in the hospital.

Meanwhile, Daddy heard from his good friend Jerry Wright, who had gone to Chicago to work with his brother Paul. Jerry told Daddy that the wages were great, so in October Daddy and a friend, Ida Lou Morris, headed up north to work at the Union Bag Company. He worked for about three years at the bag company, where he ran a die and did other chores, but he always longed to be back home in Tennessee.

About this time, Daddy got started in professional wrestling, which led him to meet Pauline Mullins, a divorcee with two young children. They fell in love and married on December 5, 1959. A brisk eight days later, romance was the last thing on Daddy's mind.

On December 13, 1959, Daddy decided it was payback

Mother and Daddy were courting in Chicago when this photograph was snapped.

time for what the state line crooks had done to him. He had been planning his return to the state line for two years. He and two good buddies, Jerry Wright and Marvin King, Jr., drove from Chicago to the state line area and exacted revenge on the man Daddy knew was behind his beating and robbing in 1957. For whatever reason, that revenge included using a fence post, which Daddy whacked into the back of the head of W. O. Hathcock, Jr.

That single incident was the beginning of the legend of Daddy's using a big stick. There was a handful of other times when Daddy would find use for a sizeable piece of lumber when going up against bad guys, but, as often as not, he went in barehanded or maybe would grab something more like a switch. That's usually all that was necessary. But his first retaliation against the State Line Mob was personal and it did, indeed, require a fence post.

Hathcock didn't take his beating lightly. He brought the law down on my daddy and his two companions. They were arrested, extradited to Mississippi, and charged with armed robbery and assault with intent to commit murder. The district attorney thought he had the goods on Daddy and his friends, but evidence from the factory, in the form of time-cards that showed all three of them were on the job the day of the incident, seemingly was proof that Daddy and his two pals couldn't have done the deed. The jury took two hours to find all three not guilty.

As it turns out, having a friend clock their timecards for them while they were gone proved to be a stroke of really smart planning by Daddy and his friends.

After the trial, Daddy returned to his job in Chicago and attended Worsham's College, a mortuary school. He continued his wrestling career on weekends. He had taken on the ring name of "Buford the Bull."

Daddy wrote a little bit about his wrestling career in an article that appeared in the December 1970 issue of *True Detective:*

> I went in training for wrestling in 1958. I wrestled in '59, '60, and part of '61 in Chicago; Milwaukee; Gary, Indiana; Pittsburgh—all over the Midwest. Later I wrestled in West Tennessee.
>
> I wasn't the best wrestler in the business, and I wasn't the worst. Wrestling helps you learn to handle yourself. Wrestling is mostly showmanship, but it teaches you how to take your falls.

By 1958, Daddy was working at a factory in Chicago and doing a little wrestling on weekends, which earned him the nickname "Buford the Bull."

You get in an old tag-team match, and they throw you out of the ring, you can get hurt if you don't know how to fall. I've had my knees, shoulders, neck all bunged up from wrestling.

The biggest audience I ever wrestled before was in Comiskey Park in Chicago. We had about 37,000 spectators, and the ring was set up at home plate.

The roughest match I ever wrestled? Well, that had to be the one in Union City, Tennessee. I wrestled Big Bill Crockett from Texas one night in Jackson, Tennessee, and he opened up a cut on my forehead. Next night I was to wrestle him in Union City.

When the referee called us out to shake hands in Union City, he hauled off and hit me with his fist. Busted open the cut he'd opened the night before. When he hit me that second night, that's when the fight come off.

We didn't wrestle. We just fought. It was a little old

Daddy and his family in the mid-1960s (from left): Carl Pusser (my grandfather), John Davis (my uncle), Helen Pusser (my grandmother), Gailya Davis (my aunt), and Daddy.

makeshift ring, and we tore it down. The referee stopped us, got some canvas and lumber and patched it up, then we fought some more and tore it down again.

I don't know how I'd got home that night if I hadn't had a wrestler named Billy Daniels to drive for me. Both eyes were swollen shut. My hands were so sore my fingers got stiff like claws. I was stiff as a board for days. It was along then that I decided to give up wrestling.

Another small sidebar to my father's professional sports career is that he actually wrestled a bear and won the match and fifty dollars. This was back when he was in high school. A summer carnival came through the area. The bear's owner had a gimmick where he challenged local boys to wrestle his black bear. Daddy pinned the bear. He later would say that it was just a little bear that didn't have many teeth or claws.

I don't really know much more about my father's wrestling career, but I've heard that as a teenager, Jerry Lawler was a big fan of my dad's. They would meet later, after Lawler himself had become a legendary wrestler. In fact, after his own long and illustrious career as Jerry "The King" Lawler, he helped another kid, Dwayne Johnson, get into the sport. Johnson, like Lawler, became a wrestling superstar as he worked under the nickname of "The Rock." Through an incredible series of events, some forty-plus years after my father became a wrestler, I was to become a friend of The Rock as he took on a movie role inspired by my daddy's story. But more about that later.

In the meantime, on January 9, 1961, on a cold and gray Chicago day a little over one year after my parents married, this little child was born. Before my first birthday, we would be back in Adamsville, the lovely town that was only a stone's throw from the evils of the state line.

The next chapter of my daddy's life was to be a truly dangerous one. He would climb into a ring of violence where his enemy came at him not with missing teeth and claws but, instead, loaded for bear with knives of steel and guns with bullets.

CHAPTER 4

Daddy's Life in Law Enforcement

In late 1961, while Mother, Daddy, and I were living in Chicago and Daddy was still working for Union Bag and wrestling, Papaw was back in Adamsville and serving as police chief. He was in the attic of his house doing some repair work one day and fell through the attic floor—and then the ceiling of the first floor. He reinjured the hip that he had hurt in the truck accident four years earlier.

Daddy drove Mother and me in from Chicago to check on Papaw. Both of his legs were really bothering him—so much so that he asked Daddy to consider taking over for him as police chief. He felt he simply wasn't up to the physical requirements of the job.

Daddy didn't immediately take to the idea of becoming police chief. After all, he had a decent job in Chicago. Papaw decided to come at the situation from a different direction. He went to Miss Joann Gibson, other city commissioners, and Mayor Leonard Blanton with his proposal to make Daddy police chief. They liked the idea. They then made a formal offer to Daddy. It was now more than just a father trying to convince his son to take over the job. It was Daddy's hometown officially asking him to do so.

Daddy liked the idea of serving his town and being near his family. The job paid only about two hundred dollars a month, but he saw it as pretty good and steady money. And there was always the chance that a carnival might come through town with a bear to wrestle for old times' sake and that extra fifty dollars.

And so it was that before I was a year old, my parents left the Windy City for good and headed to Adamsville. They set up home in a rented trailer on Maple Street.

Becoming police chief gave my daddy the direction and purpose in his life that he so badly wanted after the frustration of his medical discharge from the Marines. He enjoyed serving the public. His first patrol car was a black 1960 Chevy, a six-cylinder with a three-speed on the column. Faster cars were to come later.

Daddy was appointed police chief in late 1961 or early 1962, at the age of twenty-four. The job mostly involved watching for traffic violations and for folks getting into scuffles at beer joints that, while outside the city limits, were still near enough to Adamsville to cause problems in town.

One incident I remember hearing about was when police from Savannah, Tennessee were chasing a car full of young guys. As they headed by Adamsville, Daddy took up the chase on to Selmer. During the pursuit, Daddy shot through the car several times and also hit at least one or two tires, which caused the car to ride low. When they got to a train track, the car got stuck. And to add suspense to this story, naturally a train was coming. Daddy pulled all the boys out before the train hit the car. One poor boy had just hitched a ride with the other guys. Daddy found him on the back floorboard praying as fervently as any lost sinner.

That was about as exciting as it got in Adamsville. It wasn't until January of 1964 that Daddy raided his first still. Barney Fife probably found more real police work to do in Mayberry than Daddy had in Adamsville up until that point.

Growing restless with his job as police chief, Daddy decided to run for sheriff of McNairy County in 1964. He ran against the incumbent, James Dickey, who did not seem to have been as aggressive against the state line bunch as many people, including Daddy, would have liked. Some thought Dickey was a little too cozy with the hardened-criminal element and perhaps looked the other way regarding their activities.

This is how Daddy looked when he became sheriff of McNairy County, Tennessee, in September 1964.

In any case, Dickey would have been difficult to unseat that year had he not died in a car wreck just five days before the election. Some suspected that the state line gang arranged his death because they feared that he was going to lose the election and didn't want him then to start talking about any understandings that he might have had with them. But that scenario wouldn't have made much sense, and there was never any real proof found to support that theory. State agencies helped in the investigation. It was determined that one of Dickey's tires had simply popped, pulling the car to the right. He steered back across the road, lost control, and crashed.

Even dead, Dickey received 307 votes, but Daddy won with 3,288, while George Weatherford tabbed 3,040. The consensus was that had Dickey not died in the accident, he probably would have won the election, but if his 307 voters had gone with Weatherford, my family's life would have been entirely different. In any event, all of McNairy County, including the Tennessee side of the state line, was now under Daddy's jurisdiction.

It wasn't long before Louise Hathcock, the acknowledged queen of the state line crowd, offered Daddy first $500 and then $1,000 a month to look the other way. The bribes would have totaled far more than his annual sheriff's salary of $3,600. Maybe such payments were business as usual for her, but not for Daddy. He knew what was right and what needed to be done. In fact, his motto was, "What's right is right and what's wrong is wrong, no matter who you are." The attempted bribes only spurred him on that much more. He had campaigned for sheriff on the promise of going after the state line operations, and he was eager to make good on that promise.

Daddy soon began building his reputation as someone who was serious about fighting the despicable crimes that he saw poisoning the way of life and the lives of basically good people in McNairy County. He had *I answer all calls* printed on his business cards. And that wasn't just because he had no full-time deputies when first in office. He wanted the community to know that he took his job seriously and that all citizens could count on him. Maybe that need to help others and serve the public is genetic. I feel that same sense of responsibility tugging at me. Or maybe it's just something you develop according to how you're raised and what you observe being done by those adults who are closest to you.

Sometimes Daddy's eagerness to help people got him into trouble when he least expected. When he had been sheriff

As a rookie sheriff, Daddy, who was always a snappy dresser, wore a fedora, a thin tie, and a tiny badge on his chest that was certainly no match for his big heart.

for just a couple of months, he was driving down U.S. 45 late one night and saw a raggedy hitchhiker. He offered him a ride. Once the man got settled in and realized he had just accepted a ride from a lawman, he pulled a knife out of his pocket, stabbed Daddy twice in the chest, and dashed from the car. Daddy was fortunate that the blade had missed vital organs and major blood vessels. He drove himself to the hospital and got bandaged up. He was back at work within a day or two.

Working with the Tennessee Bureau of Investigation and other law enforcement agencies, Daddy conducted frequent raids on state line establishments, such as the Shamrock and the White Iris. The latter was a club on the Tennessee side of the line that Jack and Louise Hathcock built and that Towhead White used as the base of his operations.

As often as not, Daddy would confiscate illegal whiskey in these raids. The moonshine would be destroyed. Any legal whiskey—that is, any that was legally made but just not legal to possess or sell in dry McNairy County—was sold at auction by the state. The county would get a portion of the proceeds. In part from that funding, Daddy was able to hire his first deputy. He knew exactly whom he wanted: Jim Moffett, who had been Adamsville's chief of police back when Daddy was in high school. Jim was a good, tough man with experience, which my daddy knew he needed on his police force. Jim has often been described as a man who could arrest you and make a friend out of you at the same time.

With Jim and eventually other deputies, including the able Peatie Plunk, Willie Smith, and T. W. Burks, Daddy began building his force. He also hired Dave Lipford, another good man and the first black deputy in the history of McNairy County. Daddy assembled a solid team to go up against the state line crooks. He began his crusade against them in earnest. In 1965 alone, Daddy and his men destroyed about sixty stills.

The sheriff's department staff knew the signs of when they were about to go bust up a still. Daddy wouldn't announce it to them ahead of time, because it had gotten to where word would leak out one way or another. But if Daddy's staff saw him coming to work in his pressed overalls or an older pair of khakis, then they knew they were going to be raiding a still that day.

There had always been a little bootlegging in the western part of the county, which is also the most rugged country in the county. I wouldn't be surprised if there's still a bit of moonshining out that way today. You really can't do much farming in that part of the county because the terrain is simply too rough. So some folks did moonshining for a living. But by all

Daddy holds a jug of white lightning as he and main deputy Jim Moffett prepare to destroy a still found in the hills of Tennessee in 1965.

accounts, they were fairly nice, regular folks—not bad people like the state line crowd.

One time they went on a raid and Daddy was what they call the "flush man." That's the raider who first approaches the moonshiners, thus causing them to run toward other awaiting raiders. Daddy came up on one of the moonshiners

This was Daddy's friend, Dave Lipford, whom Daddy made the first African-American deputy of McNairy County.

Daddy and his deputies, Tommy Brown, left, and Jim Moffett, right, squat in front of a 1954 Ford that holds a still they found along with four gallons of rye whiskey.

and signaled to him to be quiet and not alert his fellow moonshiners on down the holler. The man started shaking because he knew who Daddy was. He asked whether it would be all right if he had a bit of moonshine to calm his nerves. Daddy allowed him that small reprieve. The man took a gallon jug of moonshine and began to guzzle. I don't know how much he drank, but they had to pack him out of there because he couldn't walk under his own power.

Another time, as Daddy and other raiders were coming up on a still, one of the moonshiners happened to be going off into the woods to use nature's facilities. Daddy followed him. The man had pulled his overalls down and was going about his business when Daddy eased up from behind and tapped him on the shoulder. The man jumped up and started high-tailing it out of there. The rest of the raiders caught him at the other end of the holler. When Daddy asked him why he was running, the man said, "I thought a bear done got me." And he was about right. A bear of a man had.

Sometimes the whiskey Daddy found was more mobile than still. The cars of the whiskey haulers were usually easy to spot. Even with heavy-duty shocks and springs, they would still be riding low when fully loaded with jugs or jars of whiskey. One time, when Daddy had been in office for about a year, he was directing traffic at the scene of a house fire. A man and lady in a car that was obviously hauling whiskey pulled up to the checkpoint. Daddy asked the man what he had in the trunk. The man said it was just ordinary junk. When Daddy walked to the front of the car to check the front license plate, the man hit the gas and Daddy ended up trying to dive head first into the driver's-side window. Daddy was hanging on for dear life with his left hand holding onto the windshield wipers or near the edge of the back of the hood. He was yelling at the man to stop and trying with his right hand to grab the key and turn off the ignition or anything to get the man to stop.

Meanwhile, the man was stabbing at Daddy with a small knife, and the lady was beating Daddy with a wrench. Daddy rode partially on the hood and hanging from the window for about a quarter of a mile before finally being knocked off the car. He got lots of cuts and bruises and a few broken ribs from that ride—not to mention from the fall when he let go of the car at about fifty miles per hour. The good news was that at least the firefighters were nearby to provide assistance. Daddy never caught the pair. The car they were driving bore stolen tags from Madison County, Tennessee. I think it's probably safe to say, though, that those bootleggers didn't make another moonshine run in McNairy County.

My daddy's reputation for raiding stills and chasing moonshiners sometimes provided him opportunities for playing some of his famous pranks. Here's one that Daddy's friend Jack Coffman tells.

It was fairly common for Daddy to stop at one of the local diners for an early breakfast around two in the morning. Jack and other friends would often join him. One night

Jack Coffman, right, was my daddy's closest friend. Daddy was also tight with Jack's brother Billy Mitchell Coffman (left).

three of them were having breakfast and they hatched a plan to play a joke on Jerry Coats, a good friend of theirs who they knew would be driving back from a date in Savannah that night.

There was a still that Daddy had recently found but not yet destroyed. Daddy and his friends planned their prank. When Jerry was almost back from his date, they flagged him down and talked him into getting into Daddy's patrol car with them, even though all Jerry really wanted to do was get on home. They drove along for a while and then Daddy told the group he wanted to check on a still that he heard was operating somewhere off in the woods near where they were. He pulled off onto a little road that went into the countryside.

They soon parked, and the four of them headed off into the woods on foot with a couple of flashlights. Daddy had one flashlight that he led Jerry with, while Jack and the third prankster shared the other flashlight. They went down a hill for about a mile to a holler where the still was located. When they got to the still, Daddy told the other three that they'd better go on back to the car because he would be in trouble if something were to happen to them while he was doing police business. The three headed back with one of the flashlights.

After they got a little distance away, Daddy pulled out his revolver and started firing in the air and hollering. Jerry, in the immaculate clothes he had been wearing for his date, took off running through the bushes, crashing into trees and getting whacked and scratched by branches. By the time poor Jerry got back to the car, he looked as though he had been in a fight. The other three were laughing so hard they could hardly walk back to the car.

Early in the morning sometime after that, Daddy and Jack Coffman spotted Jerry walking along the street in Adamsville when they were on their way to breakfast in Savannah. Daddy invited him along. Now a little bit older and wiser, Jerry said, "No, I gotta get home. There's no way I'm getting in the car with you."

With that, Daddy popped out of the patrol car, handcuffed Jerry to a nearby guy wire, then went off to breakfast with Jack. There Jerry still stood when they returned quite a while later. If you were a friend of Daddy's, you never were sure whether it was better to get into the car with him or not. But you could be sure it wouldn't be dull either way. They all remained lifelong friends.

Jack Coffman probably knew better than anybody what it was like to ride in a car with Daddy. He's one of the few who would regularly, *voluntarily* ride in a car that Daddy was driving. It was fairly common, especially after he was no longer sheriff, for Daddy to drive to Memphis with a buddy, often Jack, for a night of partying, which very well might have started before they left. And if Daddy were the one driving, that would mean they would be driving wide open.

Daddy would radio the Highway Patrol that he was hitting

the road and where he was going, and they'd tell him that they would clear the way for him. Daddy and Jack would party in Memphis, have an early-morning breakfast at the Steak & Egg on Poplar Avenue, and then head home. Daddy would usually make Jack drive home, even though Jack drove way too slow to suit Daddy. Jack was in a no-win situation. If Daddy drove, Jack knew he'd be fearing for his life. If Jack drove, then Daddy would be hounding him the whole way about driving too slow.

One time, after Daddy had just gotten a brand-new blue Caprice for police work, he decided to take it for a spin and really see what it could do. Late one night he hooked up with Jack and the two raced all the way from Selmer to Adamsville, which is about twelve miles. Whenever they'd meet another car on the road, which might have been a total of five cars at that late hour on that stretch of road, Daddy would flip on his blue light to make it look as if he were chasing Jack rather than racing him. This particular night, Jack's wife, Sandy, happened to be riding with him. She asked Jack how fast he was going. He looked down and saw the gauge buried at 140 miles per hour. And what's more, Jack was losing. Daddy was a fierce competitor and hated to lose.

One car Daddy owned that sure wasn't going to win any races was an old Chrysler New Yorker he got from Rod Provience. It never really suited him and had a bad engine. One night Daddy was riding around with Jack Coffman in the city police car when he decided to stop at our house to pick up this old car. Daddy told Jack to sit behind the wheel of the police car, wait about fifteen minutes, and then come get him down on Dickey Woods Road. Jack knew not to question Daddy. If Daddy wanted you to know more, he'd tell you.

At the appointed time, Jack headed out on Dickey Woods Road. To his surprise, Jack saw a car upside down in the gully beside the road. He saw that somebody was trying to kick the door open. To Jack's even greater surprise, he saw that it was Daddy. He'd somehow totaled the old car and cut his knee and scraped his elbow. The law might have been bent a little bit in the accident as well. Jack asked what happened. A little dazed, Daddy said that it must have been a blowout or something. He must have simply lost control of the car.

Daddy told Jack, "I'm injured. Take me to the hospital." So off they went to Selmer with sirens blaring. The doctors gave Daddy a few stitches. I don't know what his medical insurance coverage was, but it turned out that the car was fully covered for the accident. That sure was lucky.

Jack also tells a story about one Saturday morning about two o'clock (all stories about Daddy and Jack Coffman seem to take place around that time!) when Daddy was driving around in the patrol car with Jack in the front seat. Sandy Coffman was sitting in the backseat next to an assortment of machine guns and other weapons that Daddy kept in the car. Daddy winked at Jack to let him know that a prank was being hatched. All of a sudden, Daddy hit the gas, yelled, "Damn, Jack, there they are!" and tore out after this other car.

Then Daddy said, "Sandy, hand me that machine gun." She was petrified, but on about the third urgent request, she passed the gun up front. Daddy stuck the gun out window and Sandy just about fainted. The folks in the other car turned out to be friends and soon everybody realized the joke.

But Daddy wasn't done with his mischief that night. He asked Sandy whether she'd ever been to a jail. She foolishly admitted that she hadn't. So they swung by the jail. Daddy led the way into the building, followed by Sandy, and then Jack, who once again had received an advance wink. Daddy headed down a hall and then came to the door to a room. He opened the door. It was totally dark inside. Just as Sandy was about to enter, Daddy flipped the switch to reveal the bullpen, where all the men who had been arrested for drinking and other minor infractions were sleeping it off for the night. Sandy buried the gauge at about 140 miles per hour as she ran over her husband getting out of there.

From left, deputies Willie Smith, T. W. Burks, and Peatie Plunk stand easily in the background as Daddy fires a .38 snub nose and shades his face from the lead shavings flying back from the bullet.

I know all these stories about moonshiners and racing on country roads probably sound like something out of "The Dukes of Hazzard." I suppose that mentality of good old boys having some mildly rowdy fun was and still is prevalent throughout the country, but maybe especially so in the rural South during my daddy's time.

But everything—whether pranks, crimes, or friendships—had boundaries. Most folks knew they couldn't cross the law with impunity. Whether driving as fast as greased lightning or making white lightning, most people knew the limits and what risks they were taking with the law. Therefore, they rarely strayed into serious danger.

That was most folks. Other folks—primarily those who called the state line area home—lived on the wrong side of the law and were far more dangerous. Daddy had a different way of dealing with them.

Along the state line, there was lawlessness of every kind. The criminals would lure innocent folks who were passing by using billboards to advertise homemade biscuits, country ham, and red-eye gravy—encouraging travelers to stop, eat, and stay the night. A lot of people from up north and other places traveled that route going to Florida or the Mississippi coast. They were easy prey for the ruthless snakes who were lying in wait for their next victims.

One time Daddy got a call from a preacher and his wife who had saved all their money to take a trip down to Florida. Somehow or another, before they got out of the state line area, they were robbed. The couple came and filed a complaint. Daddy and one of his deputies then drove

After raiding a still, Daddy may be hollering, "Boys, come on out!" The bandages on his arm cover where he had a tattoo removed. (Courtesy of *The Tennessean*)

down to the state line but couldn't find the lady's purse, which was the evidence they needed. But they did confiscate a lot of illegal whiskey during the search.

With all that confiscating going on, the county eventually set up a fund to receive criminal money or proceeds from any illegal property that was seized. Much of the revenue came from whiskey. Once the contraband had been used for any evidentiary purposes, it could be sold or auctioned by the county through various legal means.

The fund from these proceeds could grow to a pretty substantial sum. The money was then distributed periodically to various county departments for uses to benefit the public good. At first, the sheriff's department wasn't allocated any of the proceeds.

Daddy eventually told the trustees of the fund, "Listen here, I'm the one out here doing all this work. Y'all should appropriate some of this money to my department. We need deputies, cars, and equipment." When Daddy was first elected sheriff, he had no deputies and almost no budget. By the time he completed his final term as sheriff, his staff included twelve deputies and a full-time jailor.

CHAPTER 5

Taking on Harder Crime
and the State Line Mob

Moonshiners who were making a little homebrew for small-time consumption may not have been Daddy's top law-enforcement concern, but they also weren't overlooked. A still was a still. But the larger mission was to cut off the big-time operators and what often ended up being a flow of cash to the State Line Mob from those stills. Even though much of the moonshine was transported out of the county, substantial proceeds still ended up in the hands of state line crooks such as Louise Hathcock and Towhead White.

Of course, plenty of alcohol—legally and illegally produced—stayed in the county and was consumed by its citizens. Whenever some folks did end up drinking too much, Daddy had his own way of enforcing the law, depending on the particular situation. For example, if he would catch some kid he knew out drinking or already drunk, and if he knew he was generally a good kid, then, instead of taking him to jail, he'd bring him home and put him on the sofa in my brother Mike's room.

Daddy would call the kid's parents and say, "Oh, Johnny's going to stay with Mike tonight." He wasn't lying, but he just wouldn't mention that Johnny was totally drunk or already passed out. And the parents might think, "Huh, I didn't know Johnny was that close to Mike." Mike would wake up and never know who might be sleeping over on the sofa. The next morning at breakfast, Daddy would have a little word of prayer with the kid. The same kid never came home twice.

The profiles of my daddy and a deputy fill the doorway of a McNairy County establishment. (Courtesy of *The Tennessean*)

Daddy would tell the kid, "I could have taken you to jail, and your parents would have had to pay this and that." If he ever caught the kid again, it wouldn't mean a sofa at our house. It would mean a cot at the jail and a different type of call to the parents.

In part, it was a different time. But also Daddy had his own view of justice. He would rather have a youth find his way to a better path than start him out with a criminal record. And he probably saw a lot of himself in kids who at times were being a little rowdy but didn't mean to do any serious harm.

Daddy treated everybody with the same respect they showed him. If somebody were creating a disturbance, say, at a nightclub, he would ease over and tell the person that he had had too much to drink and had better leave. The smart ones knew to leave and not be there when Daddy came back. The ones who weren't as quick to understand would soon find themselves going from the bar to behind bars.

Then again, sometimes a disturbance needed to be confronted head on. One instance that my friend Steve Sweat remembers is when T. W. Burks, one of Daddy's deputies, answered a call to a nightclub where there was a disturbance with about fifty people milling around. T.W. saw that there was a ringleader who was getting everybody stirred up, but he also knew that he couldn't handle it all by himself. He called for backup. He said later that he believed he could hear Daddy's car scratching rubber from miles away. Daddy arrived in world-record time.

T.W. knew to watch how Daddy was going to handle things. Daddy sized up who the ringleader was the instant he pulled up. He got out of his patrol car and calmly walked over to the troublemaker. In what was practically a single motion, Daddy slipped his revolver out of his pocket, whacked the guy on the forehead with the butt, and had it back in his pocket before anyone knew what had happened. T.W. later said the whole disturbance was over in three seconds and the man was cuffed and in the back of the patrol car before he knew what hit him. It happened so quickly and with such sleight of hand that only Daddy, T.W., and the man who was hit knew what happened. If Daddy had tried to strut into that situation and start barking orders and talking tough, something explosive could have occurred. As it was, he just defused it with one quick action. It took real instinct to know what was called for in that particular situation.

It's worth noting that my daddy didn't use a big stick in this instance. After he started carrying a gun, Daddy preferred to use the butt of his revolver to get someone's attention. Before that, he would use his open hand for a rapid slap to the head, or he'd use his fist if required. Few can say they ever saw him use a big stick. But it makes for an impressive legend. And there were a couple of times when he did indeed employ lumber to get someone's attention.

Whether he was going to use his bare hand or an implement, the thing to watch for was when he started to pat his foot and his lip started to quiver. When those things happened, you had better look out because he was fixing to pop you.

Those who knew my daddy well—such as his deputies and Jack Coffman—would say that he may not have been the toughest man they'd ever seen. There might be somebody who could say, "Buford, I'm gonna whip you," and then actually do it. But that person would want to think before doing that, because the next day Daddy might be able to wear out his hide in return. While any person can and should have a healthy fear in a dangerous situation, Daddy never let fear dominate his mind and affect his actions. That was his edge. He never started a fight, but when somebody pulled a knife or gun on him, he wouldn't flinch.

It was the same with driving. Daddy loved to drive fast as much as anybody. But there was a right and wrong way to go about it. He had no tolerance for kids hot-rodding it through the city streets or neighborhoods. To make life safer for the kids and everybody else, Daddy set up an informal racing club for kids who were old enough to drive and wanted to race.

He would block off a stretch of road far out in an area down by the river that we called Overshot Bottomdown. He would set up the racing area at night when there wouldn't be a lot of traffic and made sure the kids raced in a controlled manner. He sometimes would even drag race with them. The only rule was that if you were caught racing in a less-controlled situation—especially in the city—you were

Daddy sits in a chair downstairs in the sheriff's office of the McNairy County Courthouse in Selmer, Tennessee. (Courtesy of *The Tennessean*)

kicked out of the club. I think Daddy understood the mentality of kids wanting to drive fast and that the kids were going to do it one way or another. He thought that he might as well set it up to be as safe as possible for them.

I suppose racing seemed to my daddy like the most natural thing for kids to want to do, so he allowed it within the guidelines he established. On the other hand, he didn't have any patience for destructive mischief.

One Halloween, some kids were turning over every garbage can all the way down a street. Daddy just hid at the end of the street and waited for them to finish. When they finally reached him, he popped out and said, "Well, you've had so much fun turning these garbage cans over, why don't you just turn around and set them all back up and put everything back in?" And he stood over them as they went all the way back down the street undoing all their own tricks.

Some incidents at Halloween were a little scarier. Here's a case in point. Though Papaw was not in prime health and had had to give up his position as Adamsville police chief, he was still helping out part time with the nearby Milledgeville police. Daddy got a call on the radio one Halloween night. It was Papaw. He and the mayor of Milledgeville, who was a very old man, needed some help with a good-sized troublemaker who had just gotten back from military service. The man had had a little more to drink than he needed. Daddy and his frequent ride-along friend Jack Coffman responded.

Papaw had tried to get the troublemaker to go on home and quit causing a disturbance, but the man told Papaw that he wasn't going anywhere and that Papaw couldn't make him. Papaw could have shot the man, but he knew that was going too far. He called Daddy instead.

When my daddy met up with Papaw and heard about the disrespect shown toward his father, he got extremely angry. He and Papaw got in the patrol car along with Coffman and went to the truck stop where the troublemaker was hanging around with eight or ten other local boys. The other boys all knew Daddy, but the troublemaker didn't because he had been off in the service. The others all backed away when Daddy pulled up to the truck stop. Daddy said to the troublemaker, "So I guess you're the badass around here tonight."

The guy just sort of smirked.

Daddy asked, "Why didn't you leave when my daddy told you to?"

The man retorted, "I wasn't ready to go—and I'm still not."

Daddy said, "Well, come on then; I'm gonna take you to jail," and grabbed the man by the wrist, threw him against the car and punched him into submission. Daddy ripped his own pants leaning over to pick up the man off the ground to put him in the car. Of course, everybody wanted to laugh, but it wasn't a laughing matter. Daddy turned to the onlookers and asked, "Anybody else got anything to say about this?" Nobody said anything. As Jack Coffman summed it up, "Halloween was over in Milledgeville."

On the way to the jail, Daddy pulled over and told the man, "I'm going to make you an offer that I never make. We're going to get out and I'm going to give you the first punch. That's how mad I am about the way you treated my daddy and the mayor and how bad I want to fight you. I'm not the police now. I'm nobody. It's just me and you."

The former troublemaker, who was a good-sized man of about two hundred pounds, sized Daddy up and said, "No, Mr. Pusser, I just had too much to drink. I don't want no trouble."

Daddy was seething. "What do you mean you don't want no trouble?! You've run the eighty-year-old mayor and my daddy who's crippled out of town and announced to everybody else that you're the town badass."

"No, Mr. Pusser, I just had too much to drink."

Daddy told him to lie down in the backseat of the car and not make a peep. And then he gave the man one final warning on the way to the jail. "If I ever hear your name going out over the radio again, you won't have to wonder who's coming to get you. You'll know it's me."

And that was the last trouble anybody ever heard about involving that man.

For a lot of legal reasons, a police officer today could never use tactics like Daddy did with that man. But this is also for a very practical reason. Today you never know what kind of powerful drug, such as crack cocaine or methamphetamine, a troublemaker might be on that would prevent him from being reasoned with. But back in Daddy's early days, when it was mostly just whiskey that he was dealing with, folks sobered up and came to their senses pretty fast when face to face with Daddy.

Most law enforcement in McNairy County during my daddy's time was along those lines—just keeping an eye on rambunctious people and putting them back on the right path if they became a danger to themselves or others.

That was the case for most of McNairy County. But the strip along the state line was the opposite. It really was a cauldron of crime ranging from petty theft, prostitution, and gambling to armed robbery, illegal liquor, and murder. By confiscating illegal whiskey found on the premises of state line businesses and constantly keeping the hoodlums on edge about illegal operations, Daddy and his men made life as miserable as possible for the state line thugs.

Jim Moffett and others commented that Daddy's size, grit, and courage made for a powerful combination that the state line crowd had not had to deal with before. Daddy felt a keen sense of civic duty. He hated to see the horrible things the state line crooks were doing to people. It was also very personal. Not a small part of his crusade was payback for what the state line gangsters had done to him when they had cheated him out of his money, beat him up, and left him for dead by the road. That he had it in for them was no secret to anybody on either side of the law who knew the personal history of Daddy and the state line gang—especially Louise Hathcock and Towhead White.

By most accounts, Louise Hathcock was as tough and cold-blooded as a person could be. Some say they saw a bit softer side to her when she wasn't drinking, but that was rare. More typical of her were widely reported comments such as, "The Yankees stole this country. Every time there's one in here, I'm taking it back."

Louise Hathcock's husband, Jack, though no saint, might have had at least a degree or two less meanness and ruthlessness than Louise and White did. Though Jack was suspected of having killed at least one person, by some accounts he wasn't as quick to get involved in all the hard crime that his wife (later ex-wife) and White did. He was cramping their style.

On May 22, 1964, Louise said she shot Jack five times in the back in the room where she lived at the Shamrock Motel, which she owned. She claimed he had been beating her and had told her he was going to get a gun to kill her. She said that she had shot him in self-defense. It was her word against a dead man's, and the jury didn't have the evidence to come back with a conviction—even if it made no sense for a man to have announced to his intended victim that he was going to get a gun and come back and shoot her. And it especially made no sense that the intended victim apparently had a gun handy enough to shoot him five times before he could even leave the room.

There are many people, including me, who think it makes

The Shamrock Motel near the Tennessee-Mississippi state line. Bad things happened here. (Courtesy of *The Tennessean*)

a lot more sense that it was Towhead White who shot Jack and then beat Louise to create bruises as slim evidence to cover the crime. With Jack out of the way, Louise and White were no longer constrained by any of their own cohorts who might have had any conscience. The only obstacles preventing Louise Hathcock and Towhead White from turning the state line into their own private kingdom were lawmen like my daddy and his deputies.

Daddy and his team conducted regular raids and patrols, aggravating the state line gang as best they could with their limited manpower. But state line crimes were like an evil fire—sometimes raging, sometimes smoldering, but hard to completely douse.

On the morning of February 1, 1966, the fire flared into an explosion. A couple from Illinois (more "Yankees" in Louise Hathcock's mind) who had spent the night at the Shamrock filed a complaint with the sheriff's office stating that about five hundred dollars and some jewelry had been stolen from their room. When they reported this to Louise, she simply had told the couple to be on their way if they didn't want worse to happen. And worse could have happened, too. Some people who stopped at the Shamrock and elsewhere around the state line simply disappeared.

There's no telling how many people were robbed like the couple from Illinois. Most probably decided to go on their way. When folks did file a complaint, the evidence was always long gone by the time anybody from law enforcement could respond. It would then be one person's word against another's. During the search of the premises, my daddy and his deputies would usually be able to find some illegal whiskey to make the trip not a total loss, thereby also putting at least a dent in the robber's own cash flow.

This particular Tuesday morning, Daddy and top deputies Jim Moffett and Peatie Plunk all responded to the call, which would have been normal. They knew they would find Louise Hathcock behind the counter at the Shamrock, so they would have a tough search on their hands. Daddy had also reached the point where enough was enough with these robberies. They were going to bring Louise Hathcock in.

Up until that time in his career, Daddy didn't wear his revolver when responding to these sorts of calls. This morning, an experienced Jim Moffett said to Daddy, "Buford, don't you think you ought to put your gun on?"

Daddy replied, "Well, maybe I ought to."

They pulled over into a gravel parking lot not far from the motel. Daddy got out and strapped on a holster with his .41 magnum. They proceeded on to the motel. They arrived between 10:00 and 10:30. With Jim Moffett standing in the kitchenette between the motel lobby and Louise's bedroom, and Peatie Plunk waiting in the parking area with the couple who had been victimized, Daddy confronted Hathcock. He told her that they had a robbery complaint and search warrant and they were taking her in for questioning. Obviously intoxicated from a night of drinking that was still continuing, Hathcock stood there a bit disheveled in her stretch pants and sweater and barked, "You damn punk, I'm not goin' anywhere."

Daddy proceeded to instruct Hathcock that she didn't have any say in the matter.

She said, "Come back here. I wanna talk to you in private. I will give you the straight of the story about what's been going on. I'll explain everything about the operations down here to you. I know you've been wanting to know what's going on." She led Daddy behind the front desk to her master apartment, known as the No. 1 cabin, which was her residence. It was the same killing room where her husband, Jack, had received the five slugs in his back less than two years before.

What would soon be obvious was that Hathcock didn't want to have a private, tell-all confession about state line operations. Instead, she was trying to lure Daddy away from the protective eyes and guns of his deputies.

As she and Daddy entered the room, Daddy was surprised how neatly kept it was. She asked Daddy to close the door behind them, and he did, but it didn't close all the way because some dry-cleaning was hanging on the doorknob. As the door began to creep back open, Hathcock realized that she wasn't going to have the full privacy that she wanted. Her intentions and actions would soon be exposed to Jim Moffett in the kitchenette. She swung around as she pulled a revolver from her sweater pocket, cursed, and fired at Daddy.

Hathcock was a crack shot with a gun. Had she not been drunk and having to fire in such haste, she no doubt would have hit Daddy—and perhaps killed him, because she was aiming for his head. Instead, the bullet streaked past his left side, through the window, and into a canopy post outside.

Surprised by the shot, Daddy fell against the side of the bed and partially to the floor. As Daddy was reaching for his own revolver, Hathcock was already standing over him. She dropped the hammer on the second shot. It snapped but failed to fire. That gave Daddy time to pull his revolver and shoot. It took three quickly fired shots to stop her.

Meanwhile, Jim and Peatie both were rushing into the room, knowing that they were going to find somebody dead and fearing it would be Daddy. And if Hathcock had not been drunk basically three times over (the toxicology report showed that her blood alcohol was .28), Daddy probably would have been dead from the first shot or at least from a properly fired second shot.

Dr. Harry Peeler, the county medical examiner, arrived at 11:30. He noted in his report that he had to pry the .38 caliber Airweight revolver from her right hand. My daddy had said that she kept trying to fire the gun after it jammed and until her dying breath.

As mean as Louise Hathcock was and even though she had tried to murder him, Daddy still felt bad about having killed a woman. (You notice I didn't say lady.) It really bothered him. I guess he figured there ought to have been another way, but Louise Hathcock chose her own way.

That showdown was a scary close call for Daddy. But it wasn't without one lighter moment. As was expected, there was a whole lot of illegal whiskey found on the premises—not moonshine, but untaxed whiskey. Peatie Plunk said, "I heard somebody behind a door. I yanked that door open not knowing what to expect, and there this old fella was, more scared than I was."

The old man asked, "Miss Louise is dead, ain't she?"

Peatie said, "Yes, she is."

The man remarked, "Well, I sure could use a drink of this whiskey."

Peatie asked Daddy if it would be all right to let the old man have a drink. Daddy said it would be O.K. The man turned a half-pint up and gulped it down. Everybody probably could have used a drink to settle their nerves that morning. Everybody except Louise Hathcock, that is. She had had a few too many for one last time, and that had ended her nastiness.

The Tennessee Bureau of Investigation and other agencies gathered evidence from the scene. The McNairy County grand jury soon exonerated Daddy, saying that the shooting was justifiable and in self-defense.

Across the way from the Shamrock, which was on the Tennessee side of the state line, was the White Iris, which

The White Iris was a notorious state line site where bad things could happen to good people. (Courtesy of *The Tennessean*)

Louise had built for Towhead White. That vicious man was more than happy to continue his criminal acts and meanness after her death, but in the coming months, his ways would catch up with him. He was imprisoned at least a couple of times during the next year and a half, including a stint in Leavenworth for involvement in a multistate bootlegging operation. But being behind bars didn't entirely stop a man like Towhead White.

About a month before New Year's Day 1967, White and another inmate escaped from a federal prison in Alabama. They were serving time there for the usual bootlegging-related crimes that White was forever knee-deep into. On January 2, Daddy gave chase to two people in a speeding car on U.S. 45 at the state line. He eventually got them to pull over. Daddy got out of his patrol car and approached the car. As he got near, a woman in the front seat began firing a gun at him. Daddy was hit in the face, arm, and belly. He managed to get back to his car, and his assailants sped off. He drove himself to the hospital. A few days later, White and the other escaped prisoner turned themselves in after what I'm sure they described as just an innocent holiday for a couple of homesick "angels." Though Daddy and others felt certain White had been in the car that night, nothing could ever be proven.

I was just five years old when all of this was going on, so I don't have a personal memory of anything special happening, even on the day that Daddy killed Louise Hathcock. The kinds of memories I have of that time are things such as our family planting a sweet gum tree in our backyard. It had to be either that spring or the spring of the following year when we planted that tree. I don't really remember a lot of things that my mother, Daddy, and I did together, but I do remember that day so vividly. Daddy got hot digging the hole for the tree. Mother, of course, was trying to tell him how to do it. I saw Daddy unbutton his shirt to cool off a little. The next thing my parents knew, I had my shirt unbuttoned, too. My mother explained to me that girls didn't wear

Mother sits at Daddy's bedside in Memphis on January 3, 1967, after he suffered four gunshot wounds from an unidentified woman. Two shots struck him in the left cheek. (Photograph by James R. Reid, *Memphis Press Scimitar*, courtesy of Mississippi Valley Collection, University of Memphis Libraries)

their shirts unbuttoned. I'm sure I didn't fully comprehend why that was so at that point, but from then on I did make sure to keep my shirt buttoned.

When most people look at that tree today, they see just an old sweet gum tree. I see much more. I see my parents and me planting that tree together and then watching it grow. That sweet gum and I have seen a lot of life through the years. As my parents and I were planting the tree that spring day, I had no idea how many branches of my life were about to break.

CHAPTER 6

The Ambush of My Parents

August 12, 1967, started out as a normal day. But Mother and Daddy and I knew it wouldn't be normal. And we were right. It wouldn't be normal at all. We just were wrong about why—horribly, nightmarishly wrong.

We had packed our bags the evening before and were excited as we anticipated leaving the next morning for our big end-of-summer vacation to visit my mother's parents in Haysi, Virginia. Beyond my excitement about the trip was my great expectation about soon starting the first grade of school. There was a lot for an unsuspecting six-year-old to look forward to.

My mother, Mike, sister Diane, and I had gone to bed at our normal times. As usual, Daddy didn't get home until three or four o'clock in the morning. He often worked late because he wanted to be on duty during the times when the criminals were most likely to be active. He always said that the bad guys are not normally out at seven or eight o'clock in the morning, so he didn't need to be either. Daddy typically slept later than most people (unless he had to make an appearance for a court case) and then got up and went to his office around noon.

This particular night, as would be expected for any working person trying to get away on vacation, Daddy wanted to tie up as many of his job's loose ends as possible.

One end coming loose that night was a man who had called my grandfather a couple of times at the jail and was wanting Daddy to call him. The man said there were some things going on at the state line and if Daddy would meet him down there, he would help Daddy get to the bottom of it. He commented that he had some information that Daddy needed to know.

Well, Papaw knew that Daddy was trying to tie things up before we left on our trip, and he wasn't going to bother Daddy with a new loose end. He figured any badness would keep until we got back home.

Thinking that everything was under control, Daddy got home from patrol and went to bed at his usual early-morning bedtime. He hadn't been in bed long before the phone rang. It was the same man who had been trying to reach Daddy at the jail. He told Daddy that there was something going on down at the state line that he knew Daddy would want to take care of. He said he didn't want to talk about it on the phone; he wanted to do it in person. He wouldn't give his name, and his voice was unfamiliar.

Whatever the man told Daddy was enough to make him think it needed tending to right then. When he got up, my mother asked him where he was going. He told her that a man had called and that he was going to meet him down at New Hope Road.

My mother said, "Let me go with you, and then you can buy me breakfast on the way back." She quickly dressed in a blouse and slacks.

I think Mother thought that if she was with Daddy then maybe he'd come back quicker and we could leave for our trip that much sooner. She was eager to see her parents, and we were all champing at the bit to get on our vacation.

It was just before dawn, about 4:30, when Mother and Daddy started out in Daddy's Plymouth for New Hope Road. As usual when on patrol, Daddy had a pistol and shotgun at his side, as well as more guns and ammunition in the trunk. On this particular day, he was carrying a .41 magnum in the holster fastened to his alligator trouser belt.

As they drove, Daddy and Mother talked a little about

My mother was born red-headed Pauline Mullins. Her father was an Irishman we called Pa Jack and he worked in the coal mines in Haysi, Virginia. Her mom was a full-blooded Cherokee and we called her Ma Burthee.

going to meet the man. Daddy told her that the man who called had told him that if Daddy didn't see him by the New Hope Methodist Church, then he should come on past there and look for him at another place. If he weren't sitting out front there, then he'd be at such and such a place on down the road. Daddy said that he and Mother were talking about the trip and other chitchat and that Mother was leaning over to put a country-music tape in the eight-track player. He didn't even notice that a car, which he hadn't seen sitting behind the New Hope Methodist Church, had pulled out and was following right on their tail.

Daddy said later that when he did see the car, he wondered for a moment if maybe that was the man he was supposed to meet. Daddy sped up and the other car, a big Cadillac, sped up to pull alongside Daddy's car. There were two men in the front and one in the back. The next thing Daddy knew, the front passenger in the other car was opening fire with a .30 caliber carbine into his car. One of the first shots hit my mother in the head, and she fell over in Daddy's lap, bleeding horribly and gasping for breath.

The men in the Cadillac fired repeatedly at Daddy's car. One of the shots shattered the windshield in Daddy's face. Given all of the bullets that went in and through the car in that initial assault, I don't know to this day how Daddy dodged being hit. He took off flying as fast as he could, driving for about two miles—to a point where he thought that either he had lost the men in the Cadillac or they had simply given up the chase.

He pulled off to the side of the road to see what he could do for my mother. They were both swathed in her blood. He was just trying to do anything he could to help her. He raised Mother's head up to try to keep her breathing and to see whether he could find the wound and stop the bleeding. He couldn't find the wound, and she wasn't breathing. He knew Mother needed more help than he could provide. He had to call for help.

Before he could turn around to pick up the radio microphone and make the call, the Cadillac was back on him. This time when they fired, they hit their target. The shot blew off the lower left side of Daddy's face. Most of his bottom teeth were shot out, and parts of his left jaw were dangling down or blown off altogether. Then more shots hit my mother. If she had not been killed by the earlier shots, then these shots were certainly fatal.

With Mother lying dead in his lap, Daddy managed to drive away before the killers could finish him off. He got on the mike and radioed for help. He was on the county sheriff frequency. Papaw heard the call come across about 6:20. He immediately called Selmer police chief Hugh Kirkpatrick.

Of course, with half of his jaw blown off and many of his teeth blasted out of his head, Daddy really couldn't talk. But he was able to grunt out "help" and "state line" to where Papaw recognized his voice. He then mumbled "45" clearly enough that Chief Kirkpatrick knew which road to take. From the Selmer jail, my granddaddy put out an emergency call on all of the police frequencies.

Meanwhile, Daddy, even with his injuries and blood loss, somehow managed to keep driving. He had enough sense to know that he needed to get to the hospital, so he drove north on Highway 45 toward Selmer. He pulled into a driveway a short distance down the road, just long enough to throw some folks in the house into a tizzy. Then he got back on the highway and flew toward Selmer again, eventually stopping near Smith Store Road when he saw the police.

State Trooper J. R. Reed and Chief Hugh Kirkpatrick were first on the scene. Hugh said later that finding my parents was the worst sight he'd ever seen in his life. He had been through the Korean War, but to him this was worse. Hugh said that when he got to the scene, Mother was still lying in Daddy's lap. They couldn't get Daddy out of the car because he didn't want to let go of her. He was just screaming and clutching her as tightly and tenderly as he was able. The officers could see that Daddy was in critical need of medical treatment. The ambulance came. The crew pulled him away from Mother and loaded him on a stretcher. They knew that if they had any chance at all of saving Daddy, they had to get him to the hospital right away. They took Mother's body in a second ambulance.

Tennessee Bureau of Investigation agent Warren Jones and attorney Will Terry Abernathy (bending over) scrutinize the 1967 Plymouth Fury that my mother was murdered in on August 12, 1967. (Photograph by William Way, *Memphis Press Scimitar,* courtesy of Mississippi Valley Collection, University of Memphis Libraries)

My granddaddy was waiting at the Selmer hospital when the ambulance arrived. When the doctors, including Dr. Harry Peeler, who was also the county medical examiner, saw the severity of Daddy's injuries, they knew he needed major trauma care that they couldn't provide. They patched him up as best they could and stabilized him. He had lost an alarming amount of blood. The doctors knew that Memphis was the closest place that could provide the kind of critical care that Daddy needed. Memphis was a hundred miles away. The medical staff feared that Daddy would die before they could get him there.

The ambulance sped down Highway 57 toward Memphis. Daddy said later—and I was there one of the times he was telling this—that he stayed conscious the whole way to

Memphis. I can't imagine how he stayed conscious with his jaw lying on his chest and most of his bottom teeth left back on the dashboard of his Plymouth and everywhere else that they had been scattered from the blast. The physical trauma and pain from the wounds to his body—he would need several gallons of blood transfusions just to keep him alive that morning—combined with the horrific shock and sorrow of losing Mother, were obviously an excruciating, almost unbearable, agony even for a man with Daddy's tremendous toughness.

Don Smith, the ambulance driver, knew Daddy well and kept calling out updates about their progress. "We're at Collierville. We're getting closer. We're almost there." He was saying anything he could to keep Daddy alert and focused.

Daddy said later that, all of a sudden, somewhere close to Memphis, all of the pain just went away. (This was before people were talking much about having an "out of body" experience.) My father said he felt as if he was hovering above his dying body—as if his body was there, but his soul had been lifted right up over it. He said his life was suddenly like a film running fast right in front of him. He felt farther and farther away. He could barely hear Smith talking anymore. And then, all of a sudden, Daddy came to think, "I can't die! My children have lost their mother. I can't die. I've got to be with my kids."

Then, like a big jolt, the pain came rushing back into his body, and Smith was telling him, "Buford, we're right at Baptist Hospital. We're right here. I'm going to pull back around here, and, Buford, we're going to get you out. They're going to take care of you, Buford. They're going to save you, Buford."

CHAPTER 7

The Aftermath of the Ambush

The ambulance had sped with Daddy to Baptist Hospital in Memphis, where they stationed armed guards at the door. He had to have many transfusions of blood and a number of surgeries to save his life. He was in the hospital for eighteen days. There would be many return trips for reconstructive surgery to his face, especially his chin and mouth.

The morning of the shooting, Daddy's good friend Rod Provience followed the ambulance all the way to Memphis and waited at the hospital for the news from the doctors. He recalls, "They worked on him for several hours. The doctor came out, and I asked if Buford was going to live. The doctor told me, 'If he's tough enough, he probably will.' I said, 'Well, then he'll live.'

"The doctor then added, 'Only . . . I don't know what he will look like.'"

Rod continues, "The doctor took the broken pieces of jawbone and ground them up and made a new jawbone. When Buford came out after that first long stay, his mouth was down in a corner of his face and saliva continually dribbled out. He had to tote a handkerchief with him to swab at it. One eye also was pulled down on his face.

"We had a friend who was a dentist, Jimmy Yancey, who screwed screws down to the jawbone and fastened teeth to it."

While all of the heroic effort to save my daddy's life was going on that morning of the shooting, I was still back home asleep in my parents' bed and probably dreaming about our

This was how Daddy looked in the winter of 1967 before he had many of the surgeries to repair his face and jaw.

family vacation. It was routine for me to fall asleep in my parents' bed. At some point during the night, Daddy would usually get up and carry me to sleep in the bedroom I shared with my sister. Whenever I woke up in Mother and Daddy's bed, I knew that meant that something was wrong.

The morning of August 12, something was wrong.

Around ten o'clock, Miss Norma Woods, our next-door

neighbor, came over and woke me up. She said, "Sweetheart, you need to get up and come in the living room."

I said, "Oh, Miss Norma, something's happened again, hasn't it?"

She said, "Just come on, baby."

My brother and sister were already sitting on the living-room couch. They were just squalling and squalling. Mamaw and Papaw were there, and they were crying. A lot of neighbors and close friends had gathered. Jim Moffett and Peatie Plunk were there, too, and they started to tell what had happened.

I was so distraught over hearing the part about my daddy and how he'd been shot that I didn't hear them tell the part about Mother. I didn't hear them say that she was dead. I simply didn't hear it. Somehow or another, my mind was thinking so intensely about my daddy that, when people started wailing when they heard the news about my mother, I thought they were crying just about Daddy.

Our neighbors and friends started asking, "Dwana, do you want to go home with us today? Why don't you go spend the day with us?" The fact that my mother wasn't there wasn't unusual to me, because whenever something happened to Daddy, she was always with him at the hospital. I chose to go home with two of Mother and Daddy's dear friends, Helen and Rod Providence, because they had older kids, and they had these little scooters that I thought were really neat.

Once we got to the Proviences' house and were playing out in the yard a while, I was struck by how much all the big kids were actually playing with me. It made me feel as though I was the most desirable playmate in the world. It was almost too good to be true.

I eventually took a break from playing to use the restroom and get something to drink. Mrs. Providence was inside crying, and I asked, "Miss Helen, why are you crying?"

Before she could answer, I tried to comfort her and said, "They said Daddy is going to be O.K. They said they thought he is going to be O.K."

Of course, they were just telling us that at the time. Nobody really knew. Everybody wanted to believe.

When Miss Helen could get a hold of herself, she asked, "But honey, what about your mother?"

I said, "What about Mother? She's at the hospital with my daddy. She's always at the hospital with my daddy. She'll take good care of him."

When I went back outside to play, Miss Helen called my granddaddy to report our conversation. She said, "I've got to tell you all something. You've got to be prepared. This child has no idea that her mother is dead."

A short time later, Miss Helen came out and said, "Dwana, your granddaddy is coming to get you."

Papaw pulled up and I got in the car. Athalou Smith, another neighbor, was in the car with us. I thought to myself, "I wonder why Miss Athalou is here?" I didn't know it at the time, but Miss Athalou's daughter-in-law had burned to death in a house fire. She left behind two young girls. I'm sure that the reasoning was that, because Miss Athalou had been through a similar experience of having to tell her little granddaughters about their mother's death, she would be helpful in breaking the news to me.

I'll never forget those next few moments. We backed out of the Proviences' driveway and started up this hill over by the garment factory. We were just barely rolling along in the car when Papaw asked me, "Dwana, did you know your mother was with your daddy last night?"

I said, "Yes, Papaw, she always goes to the hospital when something happens to Daddy. She's always there taking care of him."

My granddaddy said, "No, Dwana, your mother was with your daddy when he got shot."

"I said, "Oh. Papaw, was she hurt?"

He said, "Yes, sweetheart."

I screamed, "Oh, Papaw, is she dead?"

He said, "Yes."

All of a sudden, this really loud, squealing noise just

railed inside my head. We were only a couple of blocks from our house at that point, but it seemed as though it took an eternity to get there. I'm sure Miss Athalou was doing something to try comfort me, but if she was, I was too upset and numb to notice. I jumped out of the car and I ran into the house. I locked myself in my mother and daddy's room. I lay on the bed and I cried and screamed. I could not believe that my mother was dead. I could not believe that somebody had killed my mother.

I don't even know where my brother and sister were the rest of that day. Our family had been shattered.

It would be over a period of years that, bit by bit, I would learn more of the gruesome and horrible details about what had happened to my mother and daddy that terrible morning. I would overhear a lot of it when adults, including Daddy, would be discussing it. Eventually, I would read newspaper stories and magazine articles. A lot of times, I would read the papers when nobody knew I was doing it.

At other times, the whole traumatic situation would just be thrown in my face. And as if the horrible, sobering truth weren't tough enough to deal with, it was even more painful when twisted with meanness. The cruelest way for me to be reminded of the events of that day was to be at school and have other kids say ugly things, such as, "Did your mommy really get her head shot off when your daddy was shot? Did your mother really die?" Or the cruelest remark of all, "I heard your daddy shot your mother."

Probably the least painful way—and there was no completely painless way—for me to learn more about the incident was to hear Daddy talk about it. He never did just sit down with me one on one and say, "Dwana, this is what happened." He would talk about it with other people when I was where I could hear, but he wouldn't be describing it directly to me. I would just be able to hear as he told someone else.

What's ironic is that I guess I'm carrying on that family tradition. My own kids have had to find out about their grandparents the same way I found out. I don't just sit down with them and talk about all that I know about what happened. Like my father before me, I have never talked about it with them directly, one on one. What they know is what they've read and what they've been around to hear me tell.

It's really something that's just too hard even to think about, much less to talk about—especially with your children, whom you instinctively want to protect and shelter from sadness and evil. And yet I want them to know as much as they care to know. As a parent now, I think I know how my daddy felt and why he had trouble talking with me about all that happened.

As a six-year-old, I had to struggle with my paralyzing grief and try to deal with what had become my shocking new reality. My mother was gone forever. My daddy was under constant armed guard in the hospital in Memphis, with part of his face held together by wire mesh.

Even in his condition, Daddy helped make arrangements for my mother's funeral. Through hand signals, he told my grandmother that he wanted to spend $1,000 on the funeral, which was a substantial amount in those days, especially for us. What he didn't have the capability to communicate was that he was going to have to borrow the money for the funeral. From his experience at mortuary school, Daddy knew how much it would cost to give my mother a proper funeral. Even though he was confined to a hospital bed, he was going to make sure her funeral was handled right.

My mother had a beautiful blue dress that Daddy had bought for her. He kept trying to let my grandmother and others helping with the funeral arrangements know that was the dress he wanted Mother to be buried in. Fortunately, my grandmother had been through the closet by that point and was able to describe the dresses she had seen. She went through dress by dress until she hit the one that got the O.K. sign from Daddy.

I helped pick out my mother's casket. It was metallic

blue. It would go well with the dress my mother was going to be buried in. And so the funeral planning went, with all of us trying to do our part as best we could.

Of course, the part of the funeral that Daddy had no control over was the timing. He would not be able to attend the service, because his condition was too serious for him to leave the hospital. The sadness of not being able to attend the funeral of the love of his life was a pain second only to the tragedy of losing her.

The funeral was held at Adamsville Church of Christ. I cried during the entire service. The church was overflowing with several hundred people. Following the service, my mother was buried in Adamsville Cemetery.

Daddy continued his recovery in Memphis. Childhood friend Roger Horton was a great comfort to him during that hospital stay. Roger owned Gilleys, a restaurant on Third Street in downtown Memphis.

"After the ambush, I carried a meal to him every day at the hospital," Roger remembers. "I fixed creamed potatoes with gravy and I'd always take him a vanilla milkshake. Some days I would take ground beef and chop it up real fine and take that to him. He didn't eat that hospital food. He was always waiting on me to get there with the food.

"At the time, there were some people talking and saying that maybe he killed his wife himself. When I told Buford that, I saw these big ol' tears running down his cheeks," Roger recalls. Daddy was so hurt that people could think that.

About two weeks after the funeral, Dr. Vinson pulled up to our house in his big, shiny Pontiac. I yelled, "Dr. Vinson, what are you doing here?"

He said, "I've got good news. Your daddy should be home any minute! The ambulance driver called me from Selmer. They're bringing him home and he ought to be here any minute."

Sure enough, not long after that, here came the ambulance with Daddy. I was so happy and grateful to see him.

Daddy laughs about something I must have said as we sit on the couch in our living room with my siblings, Mike and Diane. (Courtesy of *The Tennessean*)

We all were. My brother and sister and I just ran up. I hugged him and said, "Daddy, I thought you'd never come home. I was so scared you'd never come home."

He kept hugging and patting me. Then Dr. Vinson and the ambulance crew took him on in the house and got him settled in. Daddy wasn't healed back to his normal self. But at least he was home. That was good enough for me.

Daddy was horribly weak and thin, and his face was bandaged. He was hurting physically, psychologically, and emotionally, but I know it made him feel good just to be back in his own home.

Daddy wasn't home long before he realized that the best thing for our family was just to get away for a few days. He rented a little pink cottage on the beachfront in Panama City, Florida. It was a time for Daddy, Mike, Diane, and me to regroup as a family and be away from all of the attention and the horrible sadness back home. It was a quiet place where Daddy's physical wounds and the emotional pain and sense of terrible loss that all of us felt could begin to heal.

I started the first grade the following week, just like any other normal six-year-old kid.

CHAPTER 8

Back in the Swing of Things

Tennessee governor Buford Ellington offered a $5,000 reward for information leading to the capture of the men who shot my daddy and killed my mother. McNairy County citizens offered another $2,500. Federal law officers questioned suspects in seven states.

Later, Daddy was asked if he would choose a career as sheriff if he could start over again.

"If I had it to do over again, I wouldn't," Daddy told *Tennessean* newspaper reporter Charles Thompson. "When I think of what I lost—Pauline, her death. It just wasn't worth it. No, I wouldn't do it over again."

At the scenes of the crime, the FBI and other law officers discovered fourteen empty .30-caliber cartridge cases. The bullets had been soft-nosed, lead slugs. Deputy Jim Moffett found eleven bullet holes in the Plymouth.

Rod Provience told me that Daddy didn't recognize the three men in that dark Cadillac on that horrible morning, but he had ways of finding out who they were.

Daddy realized that the men who made the assassination attempt on his life were professional killers from out of state. Within three years, all three of the suspected killers were dead.

Carmine Raymond Gagliardi, a reputed mobster, was found shot to death and floating in Boston Harbor in 1968.

Similarly, in March 1969, Gary McDaniel, who was under indictment for conspiracy to murder a Mississippi

Daddy poses for a photographer in front of our house in 1969, while Old Bull sits on the porch. Note that Daddy wore his gun on his left hip.

prosecutor, was found floating in the Sabine River after having been shot in the head and back.

And George McGann was shot three times, through the heart and back, in Lubbock, Texas, on September 30, 1970. Police reportedly nabbed his killer, who wound up serving hard time, but there were still some doubts about the case.

So, who was behind their deaths? I don't know. But there are some folks who believe Daddy got to one or more of them.

As Rod Provience explains, "Buford didn't hire anybody to do any dirty work. He pretty well took care of it himself."

Two of Daddy's best friends in the whole world were Joe and Juanita Richardson, who owned and operated the Old

Home Motel and Restaurant on Main Street in Adamsville. Juanita remembers those days and how long it took Daddy to get back to some semblance of a normal life, as if that were even remotely possible.

Miss Juanita told me, "Buford's rehabilitation was very slow. He came into our restaurant before he went to his house when he got out of the hospital in Memphis. He was bandaged up so that he looked like a mummy. There were some tourists in the restaurant, and they had a six- or seven-year-old girl. His wrappings scared that child to death. I explained to her parents what had happened and why he was bandaged up like that.

"For the longest time he could only eat the very softest, mushiest stuff like mashed potatoes, milkshakes, and soups. He really couldn't taste any food. He couldn't tell hot foods from cold foods. When he drank a cup of coffee, he would sit there and put his hands around the cup. He had to drink the coffee according to the way his fingers felt the heat in the cup. Otherwise he would burn his mouth and his tongue," said Juanita.

"We served grilled calf liver with a strip of bacon on top of it, and calf liver has a real strong taste. After the ambush, he would come in here about twice a week and order the calf liver. He would say, 'I want my favorite because that's one of the things I can taste.' He said he could taste a little bit of it. He ate a lot of hamburger steak, but he couldn't taste much because the taste buds on his tongue were damaged so badly. He was just putting it into his mouth and chewing. He said that he would bite his tongue and lips and he couldn't taste anything. He said the worst thing was he would burn himself with hot foods."

Miss Juanita also remembers, "Buford liked vegetables. He loved his baked potatoes and French fries and salads. If he was in town, he would usually eat at the restaurant."

I think Daddy shared things with the Richardsons that he may not have talked about with other folks. Joe passed away in 1976, but Juanita continues to be a champion for my

One of my Daddy's favorite establishments was the Old Home Restaurant in Adamsville, which was run by his close friends Joe (seen here) and Juanita Richardson. The restaurant was the official headquarters of the Buford Pusser Fan Club, where dues were five dollars. He and my brother, Mike, also lived at the Old Home Motel for several months after a fire burned down our house.

father. She has told me other stories that not many people have heard.

"We had a room in the back of the restaurant where we had an ice machine and a couch and a desk," Juanita says. "My husband and I could go back there to take a rest or nap or watch TV. There were times when Buford would get really down in the dumps and sad. People would call him in the night and make threats and say he had killed Pauline and all of that. He would come back there and talk with Joe and me. He would cry. He was so hurt to think that somebody would say such ugly things to him.

"The way I saw Buford—he was not an abusive person. He was not a hateful person. He didn't let anybody run over him and he didn't let anybody just push him around, but he was a very kind, gentle person. Pauline had hepatitis or jaundice for a year. During that spell, she couldn't get out of bed. She couldn't do anything. Buford cleaned the house, did the cooking, and took care of the children. He loved kids."

As Daddy's body mended and the scars receded on his face and his heart, he eventually got back some of his old spirit. There was nobody better than his pal Jack Coffman to help cheer him up.

Jack recalls an adventure they took about a month or two after the August 12 ambush.

"Buford told me, 'Jack, let's me and you go to the fair down in Corinth.' Buford wanted to let folks down around the state line know that he was still in business, still walking tall, if you will.

"We might have had a drink or two before heading out," Jack continues with a sly grin. "And Buford gave me a pistol to stick into my coat just in case there was trouble. Off we went in my Corvette, which had Kentucky tags, and therefore nobody would immediately know that Buford Pusser was in it. But they might have guessed it by the speed we were going. We hit a top speed of 155 miles per hour, the fastest I ever saw Buford drive. We got to the fair in Corinth fast.

"After making the rounds and Buford making himself known at the fair, we got ready to head back. Thinking I could minimize the chances of our getting into any trouble, I made sure I was the one driving back home. What I failed to calculate was that having Buford riding shotgun was not necessarily the best way to ensure domestic tranquility.

"As we drove into the state line area, we passed the Oasis nightclub, which had just been closed because someone had been killed there a couple of nights before. Buford asked me whether I reckoned he could hit the big picture window at the Oasis. I allowed as how he never could hit anything. So Buford proceeded to pull out his .41 magnum and—*pow-pow-pow*—he put three shots into the window, totally shattering it.

"It was his first little bit of revenge against the State Line Mob for the ambush. It was merely his opening salvo as he let out some of his tremendous anger over the horrible crime and pain they had committed against him personally.

"We got back to Selmer and were sitting out in the parking lot of the truck stop having some sodas and whatnot. As usual, it was about 2 A.M. Two highway patrolmen were sitting inside the truck stop. Every time they looked out in the parking lot, Buford would stick his arm out the window and flip his middle finger at them.

"The patrolmen couldn't see who it was because it was dark and it was an unfamiliar car. All they could see every time they looked out was this outstretched arm with an extended third finger. As all of this was going on, a man walked out of the truck stop, and Buford recognized him as an old drunk who Buford had warned not to come back to town because he was always making a nuisance of himself.

"Buford yelled out to him, 'Go on home! You're not supposed to be here!'

"The fella took notice but didn't mind. This went on for a few times and finally the man headed across the parking lot to confront whoever this was that was barking orders at

Daddy smiles in his office, the stitches in his face still fresh after a surgery. (Courtesy of *The Tennessean*)

him. Buford scrooched down in the seat to make himself look small, figuring that would draw the man to his side of the car.

"Sure enough, the man sized up the situation and headed to Buford's side of the car, at which point Buford threw the door open into the man and knocked him down. As Buford got out, the man's eyes got as big as saucers. He knew he had chosen wrong. Buford gave him a lecture and a slap or two on the back or somewhere else and sent him on his way."

Daddy was definitely getting back in the swing of things. But he also hadn't forgotten my mother. After she died, Daddy began wearing a new diamond ring on the little finger of his left hand. The stones in the ring came from four of my mother's rings—her engagement ring, her wedding ring, a dinner ring, and another small ring. It was a constant reminder for him.

Not that the pain in his face and the pain in his heart weren't reminders enough.

CHAPTER 9

A Childhood Resumed

To say that our lives eventually got back to normal after the ambush and my mother's death would depend on the definition of "normal." My paternal grandmother had moved in to help take care of things at home. After a while, Diane moved out and got married. Daddy, Mike, and I tried to carry on with our lives.

It was reassuring for all of us to have my grandmother living with us. Mamaw was an incredibly strong woman with strong moral values. She always treated people fairly and would try to help others. She was a faithful member of the Adamsville Church of Christ and had definite views about right and wrong. If you strayed, she would wear you out with a switch. We had a peach tree behind the house. Mamaw would get a switch off that tree whenever I misbehaved badly, which, at the time, I didn't think was as often as she thought. As I look back on it now, she probably should have gone to that peach tree even more than she did. She probably would have, too, except the tree likely was running out of branches as it was.

Mamaw worked at several factories, including Harwood Manufacturing, a clothing manufacturer, where she was a union representative. For that reason, she took a trip to New York City for the fiftieth anniversary union convention in 1964.

She would often use her lunch hour at the factory to go to the union hall to help people with the paperwork for their

Daddy and Mamaw (Helen Pusser) pose for a photographer beside our house. Daddy's dog Little Bull paid scant attention to the celebrity photo shoot.

insurance or other matters instead of eating her lunch. She would call the insurance companies and push through the claims that were due workers but that insurance companies had routinely denied. The companies had not expected to hear any more about it, but they heard plenty from my grandmother. She also volunteered at the hospital.

I think my father got his sense of duty and of the importance of going out of your way to help people from his mother. They both believed that you didn't help people just because it was convenient. You did it because it was the right thing to do and because you saw a need.

At the factory, Mamaw could do any task—collars, buttonholes, hems, or cuffs. She made a point of becoming good and fast at every job. Even though she got paid by the hour, she had a real work ethic for not just doing a job but doing it right. When the factory later was in the process of closing down, she was one of the very last to be let go because she knew how to do every job there.

One day, my grandmother received a sales piece in the mail from a company asking her to sell Bibles. She couldn't say no to that. She started selling these big old family Bibles. They were $7.99. She sold a bunch at the factory and all over town. I still see them at people's houses to this day.

When my mother died, Mamaw saved her money and took me on the bus to Haysi, Virginia, just to make sure that my mother's family and I could see each other. She didn't want them to be cut off from me or me from them. In her mind, it was just the right thing to do.

That's the sort of stability and feeling of connection to the community and family that my grandmother maintained for us in our home. My daddy did, too. Still, the responsibilities and events of Daddy's work often overwhelmed our family life.

For example, during Christmas 1967, the first Christmas after my mother was killed, a man named Paul David English was in jail for a serious crime. He told my daddy, "Buford, my grandparents are getting old. And I'm going to

Daddy stands beside Mamaw in the kitchen as she prepares cornbread for dinner. (Courtesy of *The Tennessean*)

be going away for a while this time. Would you let me out for Christmas to be with them?"

Daddy told English that he couldn't do that because he was serving time for a serious offense and he had already escaped once. (He was the same man I told about earlier who escaped from the fourth-floor window at the jail.)

Daddy said, "I'll tell you what I'll do. You be ready on Christmas morning and I'll come get you."

English thought there was no way that Daddy would remember or follow through with that. But sure enough, on Christmas morning Daddy came and took him to his parents' house and to see his grandparents. Daddy spent the whole day with him. English never forgot that.

Early one Sunday morning a few weeks later, when English was still in the jail, a trustee slipped some whiskey in and the two of them got drunk. The trustee said, "Well, you ready to get out of here again? I still got the rope from before."

The two proceeded to climb out the fourth-floor window again and off they went. To add insult to the escape, English even took a pair of boots the trustee had been polishing for a state trooper and left his dirty old sneakers in their place. By that night, Daddy had English back in custody, but not without drama. Daddy had tracked him down in Corinth, Mississippi.

Daddy was driving his Toronado and Corinth police chief Art Murphy was riding with him when they spotted the still well-lit escapee driving by. They chased him for a good while. Then, with Chief Murphy holding the wheel, Daddy fired left-handed six times at English's car, trying to get him to stop. One bullet went through the fender of Daddy's own car, while five entered English's car. One of those went through the trunk, backseat, and driver's seat and struck English in the back. He was too drunk to feel the full pain.

To his final days, though, English had nothing but respect for Daddy, because he knew that Daddy had bent over backwards to be fair to him. If English had just stopped as soon as Daddy had started chasing him, he wouldn't have been shot.

Someone said that Daddy bent over and asked English, while he was lying on the ground beside the car, "Why didn't you stop? You know I wouldn't have done nothing to you."

These comments made English understand how sorry Daddy was that he had been hurt and that he was really shooting at the car and not him.

Daddy would treat you as well as you would let him. But when he had to, he'd use any means at his disposal to stop a dangerous situation.

Despite interruptions brought on by the demands of Daddy's job, we tried to celebrate birthdays and holidays as close to the way that we always had when my mother was alive. Daddy loved to cook—especially outside on the grill. It seemed we were always having some of his delicious burgers, steaks, or ribs. He made his own barbecue sauces, too. He would even fry bacon in his barbecue sauce. His chili was the best. And everybody loved his spaghetti sauce.

Though I'm sure he tried to shield me and the rest of our family from the concerns of daily crime-fighting, Daddy continued to go after the hardened criminal element with all of his might. After the ambush, he was more determined than ever, but also more cautious. He carried a lot more firepower with him. He frequently changed cars so as not to be as recognizable to criminals. He tended to wear street clothes rather than his sheriff's uniform. He had a bulletproof vest, though he rarely wore it, because it was made for a normal-sized man and didn't fit a man with a fifty-four-inch chest very well.

Sometimes Daddy would have a friend sit on our front porch all night with a shotgun, just so Daddy could get a good night's sleep. For my part, I got in the habit of sleeping with the TV on in my bedroom just so I could sleep. It helped drown out the sounds of barking dogs, which used to scare me because I thought the barks might be signaling an intruder. To this day, I sleep with the TV on all night.

With the efforts of Daddy, his deputies, and other law-enforcement agencies, the state line slowly but surely became less of a magnet for evil. Beginning with the death of Louise Hathcock, the state line showed its vulnerability and started to crumble. With Daddy and his men squeezing

Daddy holds a semiautomatic AR-15, the civilian version of an M16, in July 1969 beside his 1969 Ford Galaxie sheriff's car. He began carrying the rifle after the ambush of 1967.

from the Tennessee side and good lawmen such as Alcorn County sheriff Cleaton Wilbanks, who was also a Baptist preacher, and later Sheriff Grady Bingham squeezing from the Mississippi side, the state line became too tight of a hole for even the slimiest of snakes to slither around in.

Many of the honky-tonks and joints mysteriously burned. I suppose somebody collected the insurance. Others just closed rather than continuing to face the headaches and lower profitability brought about by Daddy's withering and relentless pursuit. Even though Towhead White could still wield plenty of power while locked up at Leavenworth and other prisons, at least honest folks in the communities around the state line didn't have to worry about seeing him and dealing with his evil in person.

I know now that the bitter battle between my Daddy and White was still smoldering in both men. It was continually working itself up to a fever pitch. Both men had lost women they loved because of the actions of the other man. The worlds that the two men wanted to live in were also polar opposites and were forever drawn to collide with each other. Their feud would never be completely resolved until one of them was dead. And there would be no permanent peace at the state line until that happened.

But White wasn't the only troublemaker who held Daddy's attention. It has been estimated that during my daddy's six years as sheriff, he jailed more than seventy-five hundred people. Things were getting better. The ambush and death of my mother, the lowest ebb for our family up until that time, seemed to mark a turning of the tide of crime. But with that turning tide came a dark undertow. What had already been a conflict with highly personal stakes was now supremely personal. For a while, with Towhead White finishing out yet another short sentence in a federal pen and with many of the other state line hoods lying relatively low, things were, if not calm, then at least not in a full rage.

Even if there were fewer human snakes around, there were still plenty of real ones. I don't remember which election year it was, but it might have been 1968. In any case, this is a good place for this story.

Daddy was out campaigning for sheriff, going door to door in rugged parts of a county that is plenty rural to begin with. He told Dr. Vinson that he needed a snakebite kit because he'd be walking all over the county and into some pretty wild areas. The folks at the doctor's office got him a kit. A short time later, while out on the campaign trail, he went off the beaten path and stepped over a log. As he put his foot down, a copperhead bit him in the calf. He went back to his car, got the snakebite kit, cut open the bite, and sucked out the venom.

He then went to the doctor's office to get further treatment. Eilene Coats, the nurse, didn't believe him when he told her he had been bitten. She was the mother of Jerry Coats, Daddy's friend who was often the coconspirator or victim in Daddy's pranks. She thought Daddy was just kidding around and had dropped by for a purely social visit, which he would do from time to time. But on this particular day, the doctor's office was busy and she didn't have time for more foolishness from Daddy. Finally, he rolled up his pant leg and showed her the bite. She fainted. Daddy now had to call somebody in to help not only himself, but also a fainted nurse.

Daddy was easily reelected for his third and final two-year term as sheriff in August of 1968. State law at the time prohibited a sheriff from serving more than three consecutive terms. In his final term, Daddy was riding a wave of popularity among law-abiding citizens for having done so much to clean up the state line and other crime in the county. And no doubt folks recognized the severe price he had paid to do so.

About that same time, a regionally popular singer named Eddie Bond hooked up with Daddy and wrote a song about him called "The Ballad of Buford Pusser." It was a hit on stations around the Memphis area and other country stations in the Southeast. About a hundred thousand copies of the record were sold. The first hint of the shaping of Daddy's legend and turning it into a commodity was being spun on turntables around the region. I think Daddy enjoyed and encouraged the attention. He and Eddie became business partners for a while. Eddie also had a small recording company and a nightclub in Memphis. Through Eddie, Daddy met Elvis during a trip to Memphis. They became friends.

With Towhead White temporarily out of the picture and

people like Elvis in the picture, life had to have been happier for Daddy. And then came Christmas Day 1968. It was our second Christmas after my mother's death. We hoped that it would be normal. It wasn't. Daddy received a call from Don Pipkin in Selmer. Don had already called the local police, but they had essentially indicated that they didn't get paid enough to respond to this call. "Call Buford," they told him.

Pipkin called Daddy and told him that his cousin, Charles Russ Hamilton, had been drinking heavily and had threatened to kill him. Christmas Day or not, Daddy answered all calls—much to my disappointment and despite my hopes for a normal Christmas.

Daddy knew this particular call could be very dangerous. Charles Russ Hamilton had already killed several people more than twenty years earlier, including a deputy in Mississippi and his own wife and mother. He had served time in prison as well as in a mental institution. Hamilton was still a violent and unpredictable man, especially when drinking. It was no wonder that no one else wanted to take that call, particularly on Christmas.

Daddy's real-life encounter with Hamilton was even more dramatic than how the incident was depicted in the original *Walking Tall* movie.

Daddy responded to the call by approaching the apartment where Hamilton waited. Daddy called into the house, and Hamilton yelled back for him to come in. Daddy was greeted by a revolver shot that whizzed by his head. As Daddy spun away from that shot, Hamilton fired a second shot that ripped through the fabric of his coat. A third shot hit the handle of Daddy's .357 magnum, which was still holstered, and busted it. Daddy gripped the wounded gun and, with a steely quick draw, shot Hamilton right between the eyes. Daddy had just killed his second person in the line of duty. Both times had been in self-defense while being fired upon by a drunk, cold-blooded killer. Merry Christmas.

A week or so later came the news that Towhead White had

been paroled from Leavenworth and was making a beeline for the state line. And a happy New Year.

It was accepted by everybody on both sides of the law that White and my daddy had it in for each other. White held a grudge against Daddy for having killed Louise Hathcock, as some reports indicate that she was secretly White's wife at the time. At the very least, they were lovers. Daddy and many others felt certain that White was behind the ambush that had killed my mother and almost killed Daddy.

Daddy and White had had many known run-ins. One night Daddy received a tip about a moonshine still. He went to investigate. He parked his car and went into the woods looking for the still. The tip turned out to be false. When Daddy got back to the road, he found his car ablaze. Daddy suspected White but never could prove it.

For his part, Daddy would sometimes sit in his patrol car very visibly in front of the White Iris for hours at a time just as a deterrent for any potential customers who might have thoughts of buying or doing anything illegal on the premises. It was the kind of police "protection" that hit White where it hurt the most—his wallet.

After my mother was killed, somebody shot up White's trailer late at night. White was inside and barely escaped with his life. Some thought that White's rivals from the Dixie Mafia had done it, while many assumed the shooter to have been my daddy.

Daddy and White had also had their heart-to-heart in the Hatchie Bottom that night years earlier when Daddy had forced White to crawl around in the swamp for hours while in handcuffs.

Both men had a measured respect for each other that ran almost as deep as their mutual hatred. Daddy knew that White was a dangerous man who would eventually kill him if Daddy didn't kill him first. Daddy had been pretty certain that it was White who had fired on him in January of 1967 when White and the other man had escaped from prison in Alabama.

White had been in and out of prison constantly since he had first moved into the state line area in the early 1950s. When he was out of prison, he was robbing and beating people, pulling a heist, or running moonshine and bootleg operations. He was always getting drunk and fighting, just to prove how tough he was. It was widely believed that he arranged or personally carried out the murders of numerous people. He was a bantam rooster who wanted to rule the state line roost. He has been described as ruthless, cunning, ambitious, and tough, but also charming.

White had a lot of enemies, but also a lot of cohorts throughout the South. At various times, he was a wanted man for crimes in at least Alabama, Tennessee, Mississippi, Louisiana, Texas, and Minnesota. While the state line gang and the Dixie Mafia are not exactly interchangeable labels for the groups of thugs that were responsible for crimes throughout the South during the 1950s and 1960s, there was a lot of overlap between the two groups. Most of the overlap centered on White and his cronies. He became a ringleader for the local hoods who made their living off of the robberies, burglaries, illegal gambling, bootlegging, and prostitution that so plagued the state line area.

At the same time, it was widely known that White also ran with gangsters and really nasty characters from other areas. Many of these hoods would hide out at the state line when the heat was on. Many of these people were suspected of being Dixie Mafia hit men. Many, including me, believe that it was some of these outside hit men—hired by White— who ambushed my parents and killed my mother. I know that my daddy believed it. Daddy was even confident that he knew who they were. As I noted earlier, two ended up shot dead in Texas and another was found "swimming with the fishes" in Boston Harbor.

In his best-selling book, *The Twelfth of August,* W. R. Morris (another man with whom my Daddy struck a business partnership that helped craft the image of Sheriff Buford Pusser into a nationally popular legend) described my daddy's life through his three terms as sheriff.

In this book, Morris wrote that Towhead White was shot and killed around midnight on April 2, 1969, by Berry Smith, Jr., known to everybody as "Junior." Morris's story had Junior seeing White sitting in his car with Junior's estranged wife, Shirley, at the El-Ray Motel in Corinth. Junior owned the El-Ray. White and Shirley had just returned from a trip to Alabama. White yelled a few curses at Junior and then fired shots at him with a pistol. Junior dodged the bullets and went into the motel office. He angrily came out armed with a .30-30 rifle and .357 magnum. In self-defense, Junior fired a couple of rounds at the car with the rifle. He then pulled out the .357 magnum and fired every round into White's side of the car. Shirley Smith, who had seen what was coming, had already slipped out of the car and out of harm's way.

Though Junior Smith was briefly held on a murder charge, the grand jury never formally indicted him. The shooting was determined to be another self-defense killing—case closed. Another rat had met the demise he had coming. It makes for a compelling story with a happy ending.

But speculation and rumors began spreading almost instantly after the killing. And in his 1990 book, *The State Line Mob*, Morris wrote that he believed someone else killed White—someone waiting on the motel roof. It still has the same happy ending of White's demise, but there are some who believe that my daddy did the shooting instead of Junior Smith.

I have been told that Daddy would not have anybody do his dirty work for him—especially regarding White. There are believable reports that Daddy even confided to some of his closest friends that Towhead White was the only person that he enjoyed killing.

Which version of the story is true? I guess I prefer to believe that Junior Smith took care of business. In some ways, it is hard for me to imagine that my daddy could be behind it. The side I saw of Daddy was the one of the gentle giant that I described earlier, the man who was always looking to help people in need and willing to give people who had gone a little astray a chance to get back on the right path.

On the other hand, Daddy was taking on some of the meanest and most brutal criminals in the entire country. Towhead White was among the worst of the worst. I believe that White was behind the killing of my mother. As folks where I'm from say about a vile man like White, "He needed killin'." Some people think my daddy might have been the man who killed him. I simply don't know.

But I do know this. However Towhead White was killed, good riddance.

CHAPTER 10

The Calm After One Storm and Before Another

With Towhead White dead and most of the worst criminals along the state line now crawling away, Daddy's life in law enforcement became, if not more routine, then at least less continuously tense. While there were still plenty of rough characters around, including a few who would have liked to have seen Daddy dead, I don't think he had the feeling that he was as much in danger as he had been when Towhead White was around. If that was his perception, there was always the chance that he would eventually be proven dead wrong.

Meanwhile, Daddy's day-to-day law enforcement became more routine. Of course, routine for Daddy was things like jamming his knee jumping from a railroad car while chasing a crook. When that happened, I remember that he could barely walk for days. Nothing the doctors suggested helped remove the pain and swelling. Mamaw told him that she had the cure. Daddy had his doubts, but after several days of no progress with what the doctors had suggested, he let Mamaw try her method. She rubbed vinegar on the knee and then wrapped the joint with a brown paper grocery bag soaked in more vinegar. She covered everything with a towel. The next day, Daddy was cured. Mamaw's cure was to have vinegar pull the swelling out of the knee. To this day, our family treats injuries with vinegar and grocery bags. And it still works.

For a trip to Alabama one time, Daddy needed a car that wouldn't be recognizable as a police car. He went to Rod

Provience's dealership and made arrangements to use an old Oldsmobile Toronado. He borrowed a license plate off another old car and headed down to Alabama with two FBI men on the trail of a criminal. It was late at night or early in the morning and, of course, Daddy was driving wide open. A highway patrolman spotted him. When the patrolman threw his blue lights on, Daddy just floored it and gave him a chase. Meanwhile, the patrolman ran the license tag and found that it didn't match the car.

When Daddy had had enough fun, he locked down the brakes and pulled off to the side of the road. The cop got out of the car with his hand on his gun and approached oh-so cautiously. He came to the side of the car and asked whose car it was. Daddy said he didn't know. Whose license plate

In the sheriff's office, Deputy Willie Smith talks on the phone, while Daddy looks through his files and Deputy Peatie Plunk observes. (Courtesy of *The Tennessean*)

was it? Daddy said he didn't know. The whole time the cop was also keeping an eye on the two men in suits in the backseat. He finally asked Daddy to show some identification. Daddy carefully used two fingers to pull his sheriff's badge out of his inside jacket pocket. When the cop saw what the badge and I.D. said, he stepped back and declared, "Lord, Mr. Pusser, you've aged me five years tonight." Even when Daddy was on a serious mission like that, he could find a way to have a little innocent fun.

Amid all of his law and order work, Daddy always found time to help out folks in need and show kindness.

One time, in the Purdy community near Adamsville, an African-American man was trying to get a hog ready for market. The hog got mad and bit the man in the leg and just happened to hit a main artery. The man bled to death. My daddy didn't know the family very well, but he went by to pay his respects to the family. He did so not because he was sheriff, but because it was a family tragedy in the county, and that's just the way he was.

The family was having a meal when Daddy dropped by. They invited him to stay and eat. He knew they were of modest means and didn't want to take food from them. At the same time, he didn't want to be rude or look as though he thought he was above eating with them. He saw that they had some orange sponge cake on the table. He told them how much he liked orange sponge cake and how he would surely love a slice. After he enjoyed his piece of cake and was about to leave, Daddy told the widow, "Rather than sending flowers, I want you to have this twenty dollars. I know you have a lot of family to provide for." Again, these were people Daddy didn't really know, but his heart went out to them because they were in need. Twenty dollars was not an insignificant amount of money to all concerned.

At this time, the Adamsville schools only recently had been desegregated. The man's son, Happy Robinson, was in my class at school. Happy and I had never gotten along. He would give me a hard time about my daddy being sheriff and that sort of thing. He'd act real tough and all. Of course, he had to puff up like that just for survival. I can't imagine how difficult it must have been during that time to be an African-American kid and suddenly be thrown into what must have seemed like—and no doubt was—a hostile environment of a new school with mostly white kids.

Everybody at school knew about Happy's daddy being killed, but I didn't know that my daddy had gone by to visit the family. When Happy returned to school, I got up my nerve to tell him that I was sorry to hear about his daddy and that I knew what he was going through because my mother had been killed. Happy asked me, "Did you know your father came by to see our family?" I told him that I didn't know that. He said, "And he gave us twenty dollars." He paused and said, "Dwana, I'm not going to be mean to you anymore."

More than that, Happy watched my back all through high school. I remember one time I was cheerleading for Adamsville at a football game in Middleton, which was a predominantly African-American community over in Hardeman County. Our schools were big rivals and there were always fights between the boys.

At halftime, I went into the girls' bathroom. Two big Middleton girls came in and were about to corner me. No doubt they would have given me a good beating just because I was from Adamsville. Happy burst in through that bathroom door and told those two girls not to lay a hand on me and to get out right now. As I look back on that incident and also on how the relationship between Happy and me changed, I'm amazed by how a natural act of kindness by my daddy was paid forward and created something positive for Happy and for me. That has happened so often in my life.

Another way Daddy found to help people in need was to serve as chairman and spokesperson for the Easter Seals campaign one year. He was also very involved with our local cerebral palsy fund for many years. One time he was hosting a telethon for cerebral palsy with Cousin Tuny (Doris

Freeman), a comedienne who was a local legend in West Tennessee because of her weekday TV show that ran from 1956 to 1968 on a station in Jackson, Tennessee. Daddy's being on the telethon with Cousin Tuny was a big deal to our family. I was allowed to stay up past my bedtime to watch their part of the telecast. As it got later into the night, the tote board was not meeting its goal. Daddy said, "We're going to a commercial break. When we come back, if anybody calls in and donates $100, I'll do a buck dance right here."

Well, when they came back from the break, you could see the shock on Daddy's face. The phones had instantly started ringing and were still ringing. People were calling in from everywhere. His buddies called in and were dying to see him do a buck dance. The telethon had a live band, and they started playing. Daddy began doing a buck dance right there on the stage. For those who don't know, this is a clogging-type dance that involves shuffling and tapping your feet. The crew members were saying, "I know he is dying inside right now. He is so embarrassed." He thought of doing that dance and never dreamed it would get such a huge response. From that one buck dance, he raised almost two thousand dollars in about five minutes. The phones just kept ringing. He did the telethon again the next year but didn't offer to do the buck dance. I think he should have.

Daddy had other tactics for raising money for telethons and other civic charities. More than once, if a telethon was going on and Daddy got wind of an illegal card game also going on somewhere, he'd raid the game and donate the confiscated money to the telethon. He wouldn't arrest the gamblers or even cite them. Their "donation" to the telethon served as a suitable fine for their illegal activity. They'd been warned but not arrested, and a needy charity benefited. Everybody had something to be thankful for.

I also remember seeing a newspaper article from 1970 that talked about Daddy being instrumental in getting low-interest loans for housing project homes in Adamsville. The loans allowed a lot of poor people to get on track to own a decent home. He never really talked about his involvement in that kind of thing at home. Over the years, folks have come up to me and told me how Daddy helped them out in one situation or another with an act of kindness. I would also occasionally come across an article because my grandmother kept just about every newspaper clipping she could find about her son. She was so very proud of him.

As Daddy's third term was winding down in the summer of 1970, the campaign to replace him was heating up. Several good men were running, but for Daddy there was no question about whom to support. He backed Jim Moffett, his longtime chief deputy and right-hand man. Jim didn't win. The election went to Clifford Coleman, who had been sheriff years before. In a nice tip of the hat to Daddy, the voters in our little town of Adamsville elected him constable. He hadn't even been on the ballot. Being constable meant that he could officially keep a few of the perks and ties to law enforcement, such as carrying his gun and a police radio, and he could use his car as an official vehicle.

There had been a lot of speculation around McNairy County and really throughout the state that Daddy might run for governor of Tennessee on the Republican ticket. Several political leaders were pushing for it. The man Daddy backed in the Republican primary lost to Winfield Dunn, who was also a good man. Daddy threw his support behind him and actively campaigned for him. After Dunn surprised many people by beating the better-known John Jay Hooker in the general election, Daddy had hoped to be appointed an assistant state safety department commissioner in the Dunn administration, but that didn't come through.

Adamsville and McNairy County ironically would have their first native son serve as governor of Tennessee just four years later, when Ray Blanton was elected. Unfortunately, he didn't last a full term. He was thrown out three days before his term was over because he had paroled an unusually high number of prisoners in the last days of his administration—even after three members of his staff had been arrested for taking bribes in exchange for paroles. Blanton later was convicted of selling liquor licenses to a friend while in office and served almost two years in prison. But that's another story (and book and the resulting 1985 movie called *Marie,* featuring Tennessee lawyer, future U.S. senator, and eventual Republican presidential hopeful Fred Thompson in his first movie role, as himself), so I'd better not get into that can of worms here.

Back on topic, my friend Steve Sweat reminded me of this story that happened not long after the 1970 election. W. T. Yarborough, one of Daddy's best deputies, figured that the new sheriff would want to bring in his own deputies, so he went to work for the Selmer Police Department. W. T. got a call over the radio that a suspected drunk driver was coming up Highway 45 from the state line. W. T. then spotted the car, with three men in it. He fell in behind them going down the road. At that time, W. T. weighed only about 160 pounds. He was just a young, slim black man about to confront a car full of drunken good ol' boys from out of state.

The Selmer dispatcher suggested that W. T. wait for back-up before pulling them over, but, though nervous, W. T. radioed back that thought he'd be all right. He pulled the car over. The driver was a big guy with snuff all over his beard. Two similar men piled out of the other side of the car. W. T. was starting to get a little more nervous. "Whaddya stop me for?" the driver growled.

"Well, we had a call on you. I need to see your license," W. T. responded to the obviously drunken driver. "I'm afraid I'm going to have to take you in."

"You and who else?" the driver snarled.

About that time, W. T. said he could hear a big rumbling coming up behind him. He turned around and saw Daddy's big white Ford. He said he was never so relieved to see somebody in his life. Daddy stepped out and asked, "W. T., need any help?"

W. T. was feeling a whole lot less like a scared Barney Fife at this point and said, "No, thanks, Buford. Everything's under control. I think I can handle it."

The driver whispered to W. T., "Is that Buford Pusser?"
W. T. confirmed that it was.

"Where do you want us to go?" They all loaded into the back of W. T.'s cruiser and off they went to the jail.

I think that story shows how, even after Daddy wasn't sheriff anymore, he still watched after his fellow officers and the people of McNairy County. There's no telling how far he had to drive to get there to back up W. T. Yarborough that day. And there's no telling what might have happened if he hadn't gotten there when he did.

Sometimes the heated situations my Daddy faced were hotter and closer to home—in fact, a *lot* hotter and right at home. No night was hotter than the cold one in the fall of 1971 when our house burned to the ground.

I wasn't staying at home that night. My grandmother was at a union meeting in Nashville, and I was spending a couple of nights out of town with a friend. Daddy and Mike were "baching" it at home by themselves. Because Mamaw wasn't there to do the laundry, Daddy had put a load of clothes in

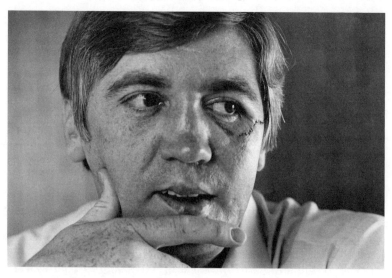

This is a shot of Daddy after he had eyelift surgery. (Courtesy of *The Tennessean*)

the dryer and had lain down across his bed. He thought if he just lay across the bed instead of going to bed, then he'd wake up. He was then going to take the clothes out and wash another load. He did wake up, but by the time he did, the house was on fire.

Fortunately, not too long before this fire, Daddy had bought fire detectors. But back in those days, fire detectors were not like the smoke detectors now. The house had to be really flaming for things to get hot enough to melt the part of the alarm that would make it sound. It got that hot this night. When the siren went off, Daddy and Mike both instantly woke up.

What had happened was that the dryer had stopped turning but had kept getting hotter and eventually caught the clothes on fire. We had been having a problem with that dryer, but we thought it had been fixed.

A complicating factor was that Daddy stored his ammunition in the utility room where the dryer was. When the siren woke Mike up, the next thing he heard was the sound of bullets exploding in every direction from the utility room. When he heard that and smelled the smoke, he just knew that our house was under assault and that somebody was trying to kill Daddy and anybody else in the house. He crawled under his bed to hide.

Daddy ran down the hall toward Mike's room hollering, "Mike! Mike! The house is on fire! Get out! Get out!" When Daddy looked into Mike's room, he didn't find him, but fortunately he saw Mike's foot sticking out from underneath the bed. He pulled him out and yelled, "Son, the house is on fire! We've gotta go now!"

Mike asked, "Are they shooting at us?"

Daddy said, "No, that's my bullets going off. Get some clothes and come out."

Mike turned around and grabbed his football uniform. They had had a football game that day. Mike took off with it. He didn't get anything else, bless his heart.

Mike laughed about it later, but of course he was mad at

himself because he was such a jock and a macho man. But anybody would have panicked. We all felt that Daddy and Mike were lucky to get out alive and unhurt at all.

I didn't find out about the fire until the next morning at breakfast. My friend's father told me, "First of all, I want you to know everybody is O.K., but your house burned last night."

My mind just began racing. After everything else I'd been through, now our home had burned. I wanted to make sure that Daddy and Mike were all right.

He told me, "Yes, your daddy and Mike are O.K." He said, "Your daddy called me early this morning, about four or five o'clock, and wanted us to know what happened."

The house was a total loss. My uncle Bill, husband of Daddy's sister, Gailya, brought a bulldozer and other equipment over from his grading company near Memphis and razed the house. He also dug a hole for a basement, because Daddy knew he wanted a basement in the replacement house. The basement would basically be his bedroom area.

Another generous gesture came from Elvis Presley. When Elvis heard about the fire, he quietly sent $1,000 to help rebuild the house. That was back when $1,000 was real money, even to Elvis. He insisted that Daddy accept it. Daddy did so gratefully, recognizing the spirit of friendship in which it was given. The money was especially helpful because we had recently added a den and bedroom on the house, but the insurance hadn't been increased to cover the extra footage.

Elvis would always be welcome at every door to our new house. As it turned out, that was saying a lot. The new house ended up having seven exterior doors, an unusually large number for a house that was not all that big. The reason was that Daddy realized that the old house could easily have been a fire trap. There was no door at all in the end of the house where Mike's bedroom was. But the new house had at least one door just a few feet from almost any point in the house.

Daddy also added a special feature for my bedroom. Knowing that I was fearful of people breaking into our house, he made the windows in my bedroom, which was on the front side of the house, start extra high from the ground. They let in plenty of sunlight but provided me with the reassurance that nobody could see in or get in through them. Of course, with all of those extra doors, a prowler wouldn't have needed to use a window. I'm glad I didn't think about that at the time.

While the house was being rebuilt, I lived with Mamaw and Papaw at their house on Baptist Street. It was already my home away from home because we ate a lot of our meals there and I would spend lots of nights there, especially in the summer. Mamaw really had her hands full with her regular job and basically running two households.

Daddy and Mike stayed with Juanita and Joe Richardson at the Old Home Restaurant and Motel on Main Street. For years, the Old Home Motel had been like Daddy's second home, and Juanita and Joe were like second parents to him. Daddy would always stop by and say hello to them whenever he was coming back from a trip and often just when he was passing by. Joe has passed away, but the Old Home is still there and Miss Juanita works the front desk with her companion, a big, old gray cat.

To this day, tourists come by the Old Home and say they want to stay in "Buford's room." I guess it's not exactly the average tourist who asks for the room but the real history buffs. Miss Juanita doesn't mind one bit. After all, she founded the first Buford Pusser Fan Club back in the 1970s.

The Old Home wasn't the main tourist mecca for fans of my father. After *Walking Tall* came out, our house was ground zero. It's now an official landmark and museum, but the tourists and the curious came by even when we still lived there. And they found an eager tour guide in my grandmother.

I can tell you about my grandmother being a willing

accomplice to tourists and also the importance of the basement addition to our house with a single story.

One of the main reasons why Daddy wanted the basement was so that he could have his own private area with a bedroom, bathroom, and small living room. It was basically like a hotel suite. It was ultra-private and had no windows or way to get in other than the door at the top of the stairs. Daddy told Mamaw, "Mother, you keep bringing all these tourists into our living room. I need some privacy where I can get away."

One particular morning, some tourists came by and were just busting for a chance to meet Daddy. They were such big fans, and of course Mamaw was just beaming with pride that these folks thought so much of her son. She said, "I'll tell you what. He's downstairs asleep. If you all want to wait till he wakes up, you're welcome to. Just sit down over there on the couch. He'll be up sooner or later. I don't know when. It's usually about noontime."

Anybody who was as enthusiastic about Daddy as these folks were would naturally be more than happy to wait. Mamaw went on about her business in the kitchen and offered them a Coke. She probably even fed them something since it was about lunchtime.

Sure enough, after a while, they heard Daddy stirring around and starting up the stairs. Everybody got quiet with anticipation for the entrance of the legendary Buford Pusser. The door flew open and who should appear but the great Buford Pusser . . . in his tighty whities!

Daddy slammed the door and hollered, "Mother!"

She hollered back through the door, "Well, if you didn't want people to come by and see you, you shouldn't have let them make that movie about you and make you famous. Put your clothes on and get back up here!" He eventually did. That stairway was the only way out at that time.

Later on, as he got more money, Daddy added a garage on the back of the house next to where his bedroom was. There had been just a carport at the side of the house, but that didn't work out because people could tell when he was home—tourists and bad guys alike. If folks knew he was home, he couldn't get any rest. He had gotten to where he parked his car on a gravel road a block away and then walked home, all so folks couldn't see just by passing by that he was home.

On at least one occasion, though, my Daddy probably wished he didn't have that garage. One Saturday afternoon, he pulled his big black Ford LTD out to wash it in the driveway. It must have been a spontaneous notion because he hadn't bothered to change out of the slip-on dress shoes that he was wearing. When he finished washing the car and getting it all nice and shiny, he pulled it back in the garage. As he moved his foot from the gas pedal to the brake, his wet foot slipped off and the car just plowed right into the back wall of the garage. The car, which was built about like a tank, showed little damage. But the garage wall and the ego of the car's famously expert driver both suffered considerable stud damage.

Whether Daddy's car was hidden down the road, parked in the driveway, or resting in a wall, folks kept knocking on our door, and my grandmother kept letting them in.

Part of the reason my grandmother wouldn't turn away a stranger was her religious faith. She was a firm believer that you never could know whether the person knocking might not be in a situation comparable to Joseph and Mary looking for room at the inn for the birth of Jesus. Or maybe it would be like the situation in "The Christmas Guest," the classic Grandpa Jones story where three needy strangers come knocking at a man's door three separate times one Christmas. The man welcomes each one and finds out later that it had been Christ each time.

My daddy's version of Christian charity didn't involve quite that much hospitality. I know few people who have that much faith when you get right down to it. But my grandmother was a special person with an extraordinary faith in God and in people. Her faith in the former never failed her, but her faith in the latter would one day allow great darkness into our home.

In the meantime, we enjoyed our new home and the interesting things that happened because of Daddy's celebrity. There would be records, a best-selling book, numerous awards, and countless articles. Even "60 Minutes" would do a story about Daddy's career. But none of that really prepared us for the emotional mountains and valleys that lay just beyond.

CHAPTER 11

Walking Tall, the Movie

My daddy was a hero to me just for being my daddy. He was a hero to some in our small part of the world for cleaning up some really bad places. In 1972 something happened that made Daddy a hero to the world, and that was the making of the feature film *Walking Tall.*

I've probably watched the film fifteen or sixteen times since its premiere on February 22, 1973. The older I've gotten, the less I've watched it. I probably went for fifteen years without watching it at all. It has just gotten harder to look back on some of those violent times as I've grown older.

Walking Tall proved so successful that it spawned two movie sequels, a TV movie, a 1981 NBC-TV series, and another feature film in 2004. But I have tried not to get too caught up in the world of moviemaking because I've found that I have to live in the real world and deal with what goes on day to day.

The first time I saw *Walking Tall* was at the State Theatre in Henderson, Tennessee, with my daddy. We sat in the back row. When it got to the part where my mother was killed, Daddy got up and went out to the lobby. In a few minutes, I got up and went out there to be with him. He stood looking out the window. It was daytime and the light seemed to silhouette him. I went over and put my arm around him, put my cheek to his stomach, and cried, "Daddy, it's O.K., it's O.K.!" It was doubly hard on him to

This shot captured Daddy in front of a phony still on the set of *Walking Tall*. Notice how he kept his wallet in his front pocket.

see that horrible memory on the movie screen after he had already lived through it and was still haunted by it.

The film was quite obviously based on my daddy and what happened to him because of his battle with the state line gang. While my father's exploits have become legendary, the truth is that most of the days he spent as a lawman were relatively quiet. The legend was built on events that took place on only a few days of his six years as sheriff. The film *Walking Tall* magnified Daddy's exploits just that much more.

But the film might have never been made at all had it not been for Mort Briskin. It was just by accident that the Hollywood businessman heard the story.

Briskin had the TV on while he was shaving. He heard the "60 Minutes" interview with Daddy. He stepped out of the bathroom and watched it. He called his secretary and said, "Find this man. Get in touch with this man. I want to talk to him!"

When Briskin called my father, Daddy thought it was a big joke. "Yeah, right," he said with a laugh. "You really want to make a movie about me."

And Briskin was trying to explain, saying, "I'm very, very serious."

Of course, at that time, there were no fax machines or personal computers with e-mail capacity, so Daddy asked Briskin to send him a Western Union telegram in Savannah, Tennessee. "I want to see if you're legitimate or not," he told him.

An hour or two later, Daddy got a telephone call from the man with the local Western Union office.

"Buford, you're not going to believe this. I got a message from a man in Hollywood, California, and they want to make a movie about you."

Daddy asked, "Are you sure it's from California?"

He said, "Yes, I've got it right here in my hand."

Daddy drove over to the Western Union office and got the telegram. He then called his good friend Jack Coffman and said, "Jack, you're not going to believe this, but somebody's wanting to make a movie about me. Isn't that hilarious?" He really thought it was just a big joke.

When Daddy was able to verify that both the message and Briskin were legitimate, he called Jack back and said, "You're not going to believe this. These people are real."

Once it sank in, he was excited and amazed.

This is how Daddy appeared on the CBS-TV show "60 Minutes" when Roger Mudd interviewed him in 1969. This piece attracted the attention of Hollywood producer Mort Briskin and inspired him to turn Daddy's experiences as a lawman into the movie *Walking Tall.*

First, Mort Briskin and fellow producer Charles Pratt from Bing Crosby Productions flew to Tennessee to talk with Daddy. Then Daddy flew to Los Angeles to talk with them some more. They drew up the contract. Daddy didn't have a lot of money and knew nothing about movie deals. He contacted Lloyd Tatum, who was considered to be one of the smartest attorneys in our area. Tatum put together a deal that would pay Daddy 7 percent of the movie's box-office receipts. The lawyer was to get twenty-five cents of every dollar that Daddy received.

The movie eventually did a worldwide box office of something like fifty million dollars. We probably altogether over the years got a little over a half a million dollars from the movie company.

Texas native Joe Don Baker took on the starring role of my daddy in *Walking Tall* and was great as far as Daddy and I were concerned. But at one time, Briskin had been negotiating with Robert Mitchum to play Daddy. I think the main reason why Mitchum didn't work out was that Briskin needed an actor who could star in the movie and also in a possible follow-up TV series. Mitchum was a movie star, and he wasn't going to have the time or desire to work on a TV series.

Once the script was written, the producers and director checked out locations for filming in and around our hometown. Daddy was really excited that it was going to be made in the places where the story actually took place. But other folks had other ideas.

Certain local politicians were determined that *Walking Tall* would not be filmed in McNairy County. They told the Hollywood guys, sorry, McNairy County is not available. It was purely a matter of jealousy. Daddy told them, "Fine. I'm going to take the movie to Chester County and Madison County."

He did exactly that, and those neighboring counties welcomed the production company, cast, and crew with open arms.

Most of the movie was filmed in Chester County and its county seat of Henderson, while other scenes were shot in Jackson in Madison County. The officials in these counties were most grateful and said, "Please come here."

The cast and crew stayed in the local hotels and ate in the local restaurants. They spent thousands of dollars to remodel the courthouse in Henderson, and I'm sure they spent several hundred thousand dollars at the local businesses.

Of course, Mamaw wasn't impressed by anyone just because they were from Hollywood. When the top guys came to Adamsville, Daddy wanted to treat them to some Southern hospitality and country cooking. Mamaw didn't feel quite the same way.

Daddy invited producer Charles Pratt, his wife, and Floyd Joyer, a production man, over for lunch one afternoon.

Well, my grandmother didn't like the movie people. Her attitude reminded me of the way Granny on "The Beverly Hillbillies" sometimes treated the banker, Milburn Drysdale, and his wife. Mamaw was just plain ol' ornery and resistant to Daddy's idea.

She didn't even like the idea of the movie. As time went on, we found out why. Mamaw didn't like the looks of Lurene Tuttle, the actress the producers had picked to play her.

My grandmother was very tall and slender. Lurene Tuttle was short and a little bit round. She was an extremely accomplished actress, but my grandmother was so mad. She was very prideful and felt as though she was being stereotyped as a little old Southern granny.

Anyway, Daddy told her, "Mother, you're going to make them lunch."

Mamaw was about to prepare them chicken and dressing, and Daddy said, "I want you to make dumplings."

Mamaw was too stubborn not to make what she wanted, so she made both dishes.

Now, almost always you have dumplings with chicken, but Mamaw, continuing to be obstinate, thought, "Humph! I'm not making chicken and dumplings."

She made ham and dumplings. She was just pouting the

whole time. And there they were at the table, while she was back over in the corner of the kitchen as if she were the maid.

She told Daddy, "I guess you want me to be your maid and serve everybody."

He said, "Mother, I just want you to be a hostess. We're having them in our home."

I never will forget that meal. Charles Pratt's wife asked, "Oh, Mrs. Pusser, could I have some more of those delicious chicken and dumplings?"

And Mamaw said, "They're not chicken and dumplings! They're ham and dumplings, and if you can't tell the difference, no! You can't have no more of them!"

Whoo! My daddy looked at her, and sternly said, "Mother!"

She retired to her bedroom to pout. Of course, Daddy got some more dumplings for them. But Mamaw was always that way. She never liked the movie or either of the sequels.

Oh, by the way, for dessert Mamaw made them her specialty, 7-Up cake. When anybody died or they were having potluck at work and everyone was supposed to bring a dish, Mamaw would bring her 7-Up cake. She was famous for it.

Back to the filming of *Walking Tall*. The courtroom scenes were filled with people from Henderson and Chester County. Lloyd Tatum, Red West, Jason Hollingsworth, all locals, got small speaking parts. (In the second *Walking Tall* movie, I was in the crowd during a racing scene where the character of my daddy busts out a windshield.)

Several local clubs and honky-tonks got free facelifts, courtesy of the movie. The Delta Club, outside of Jackson, was reborn as the Lucky Spot for the movie, and the Pine Ridge Club, between Jackson and Bolivar, got a makeover.

A number of scenes were also filmed in some of the small rural communities, places such as Medina and Sweet Lips.

Daddy poses with actor Bruce Glover, who played Deputy Grady Coker, in front of a fake still on the set of *Walking Tall*.

A preproduction party was held at the Holiday Inn in Jackson. Daddy had a lot of his friends and political supporters as guests. It was there as a twelve-year-old girl that I first met and got to know Joe Don Baker, the movie star who played my daddy. He was so good and kind to our family. Years after my daddy's death, he still sent Christmas presents and cards to me. We stay in touch to this day.

Daddy and Joe Don became very good friends. They shared many of the same ideals. They were buddies. When Daddy went out to California, he sometimes stayed at Joe Don's house. Daddy worked as technical adviser on the film and also helped Joe Don on the script. I believe that was one of the reasons why Joe Don didn't act in the second *Walking Tall* movie. They changed the script for the sequel, which my daddy had helped write.

Daddy and Joe Don had a lot of similarities. Some people say Bo Svenson, who portrayed Daddy in the sequel, favored Daddy more physically, but I know Daddy and Joe Don Baker were more alike.

As for other cast members, I got to know the child actors who played my brother, Mike, and me. They were real-life brother and sister Leif Garrett and Dawn Lyn. The last time

Hollywood movie men celebrate with Daddy at the preproduction party before *Walking Tall* began filming in West Tennessee. From left are Floyd Joyer, director Phil Karlson, Daddy, Vally Hill (manager of the Holiday Inn where the crew stayed), and producer Mort Briskin.

Daddy and actor Joe Don Baker, who played my father in the original *Walking Tall* film, share the big stick in a publicity photo for the movie.

I watched the movie, it was amazing to me how much Dawn looked liked my oldest daughter, Atoyia.

We were pen pals for a while. We played on the set. Leif was about my age, and Dawn was nine during the filming of the first movie. Their mother was a really sweet lady. One day on the set, I said to her, "Boy, I sure am sweating."

She told me, "No, dear. Ladies don't sweat. They dew. You're not sweating. You're dewing."

I remember one day on the set when I was aggravating Papaw. I was standing on the tailgate of his pickup truck. Papaw had told me two or three times to get off because I would hurt myself. One of the men with the makeup department called me over. He dressed up my arm to make it appear that it was hurt pretty badly. It was horrible looking. He told me what to do next and I gladly obeyed.

I hopped back up on the back of the truck and hollered, "Hey, Papaw, watch this!" Then I jumped off and screamed as if I had gotten hurt.

And Papaw yelled, "Oh my gosh, somebody get a doctor!" Then he saw that I was laughing. That got me into trouble. I got a bad whipping over it, but it was worth it for that Hollywood moment . . . I *think!*

Watching the actors make the movie was interesting. At the time, it was hard to comprehend that it was about our lives, until I saw it at the theater. As Daddy said when interviewed at the time, about 80 percent of the first film was accurate. But a whole lot of things were dreamed up for drama's sake.

Though it is true that Daddy was beaten up and left for dead after his trip to the state line, he never caused a local sheriff to have a car crash, much less saw it explode and kill the officer. And he never moved a judge's chamber into a courthouse bathroom, though he did threaten to one time. The film depicts him as having seven deputies on his first day in office, but he actually had none.

And in the violent sequence where the bad guys kill our German shepherd and shoot out the windows in our house, there was an incident where some men killed our dog, but our home was never fired upon.

As for my mother's funeral scene, where Daddy showed up with a cast on his chin and then joins the children in the funeral procession, Daddy wasn't home for Mother's funeral because he was in the hospital for more than two weeks after the ambush.

And in the finale of the film, there's the big crash scene where Daddy drives the car through the doors of the Lucky Spot. It didn't happen—though Daddy did shoot out the window of the Oasis Club that time. The screenwriters probably couldn't resist the chance to get in one more good car crash.

Of all the things blown out of proportion, the most significant has to be "The Stick."

Daddy always kept a nightstick in his car. A couple of times he had also used switches on people. Once or twice, he might have picked up a fencepost or a stray two-by-four before he walked into a tavern full of rowdies, but that was because he didn't have a gun on him or didn't want to use it if he did.

Nevertheless, when you mention the movie *Walking Tall* and Buford Pusser, "The Stick" is what most people remember. Since that stick has become such a powerful, lasting image, I guess it's a good thing that Mort Briskin came up with it.

Let me make the point loud and clear here for the record. Daddy never carved his own big stick, and when he was sheriff, he didn't go around busting people up with one. He may have used his fists or the butt of his gun, but rarely a stick. On those rare occasions when the situation called for a stick, he always seemed to find one just the right size nearby.

Of course, there is one good story about a man Daddy went after with a piece of wood that was bigger than a true switch—but still smaller than a big stick. Let's just call it a small tree limb. Anyway, this man was known as Flagpole. He would get drunk, start threatening his family, and generally just be "acting a fool" and be a nuisance. He truly disturbed the peace and often endangered everybody around him.

Daddy hoists two big sticks—one a promotional stick, and the other a gift from a fan. He signed many big sticks for fans at promotional events after the release of *Walking Tall.* (Courtesy of *The Tennessean*)

This particular time, he was even drunker than usual and making threats. His wife called for help and my daddy responded. She told Daddy that Flagpole was in the family's outhouse and had a gun. On his way to the outhouse, Daddy tore a large switch off a tree. He hollered, "Flagpole, come out of there or I'll come in after you."

Flagpole yelled back, "I'll shoot you."

With that, Daddy jerked the outhouse door open, yanked Flagpole out of the outhouse, and proceeded to whip him with the big switch right in front of his entire family. Daddy then hauled Flagpole off to jail.

Early the next morning, Daddy went up to the jail. He brought Flagpole out of his cell to have breakfast at the little yellow-topped metal table where Papaw and other jailhouse workers would eat. They were just two men sitting there at the table and having breakfast. At some point, Flagpole asked Daddy, "Buford, why did you whip me in front of my family with that switch? Why did you humiliate me in front of my family?"

Daddy said, "Flagpole, you're right. This time I did whip you like you were a little kid. If I ever hear of you behaving like this again—getting drunk and beating on your wife and children or anybody else—I'll use something bigger than a switch and whip you like a man. And Flagpole, you don't want me to do that." In other words, if there was a next time, Daddy and Flagpole wouldn't be having breakfast together at that little yellow-topped metal table the next morning.

Many years later, I met Flagpole's daughter at a church function. I had not seen her in so long that I didn't even know who she was. She made a point of introducing herself and then told me how grateful she was for what my daddy had done that day. She said her daddy was a changed man after that thrashing and lecture Daddy had given him. He became a good husband and father.

Other than when Daddy got his revenge with the fence post on W. O. Hathcock at the Plantation Club back before he was ever even police chief, the incident with Flagpole is about as close to a real-life "big stick" story as there is to tell about my daddy.

Still, when Daddy did publicity for the movie and after he was out of office, he knew that people liked the image of the stick, so he carried a stick around with him. People loved that for its symbolism.

So, the stick stuck, and there are several in Adamsville today. One stick that was used in the movie is now in the Buford Pusser Museum, and there's one on display that was a lead pipe disguised as wood because the wooden one that Bo Svenson used wouldn't break the windshield. And there's a newer stick that I'll tell you about a little later.

As for the film itself, I think Daddy liked the movie fine. He was pleased with the job done by director Phil Karlson, who had directed several films about organized crime, including *The Phenix City Story*. He brought a good feel for the material and tone of Daddy's story. I think *Walking Tall* moved Daddy more emotionally than he thought it would. But he would not have liked the two sequels. They were a little more Hollywood. No doubt the films would have been different if Daddy had played himself as planned, or even if Joe Don Baker had played the role.

My grandmother was probably the toughest critic in the family. As I said before, she never liked the lady who played her in the movie. Mamaw was very slim, five foot ten, and dark headed. Actress Lurene Tuttle was short and wore her hair in a bun. My grandmother simply was not a granny type at all. She was a union leader and a mover and a shaker in the community.

I never heard Papaw complain about Noah Beery, Jr., the actor who played him on the screen and who was soon to be beloved by TV audiences for his portrayal of Joseph Rockford on "The Rockford Files." But my grandmother never liked the lady chosen to play her, and she was very vocal about it. (If you don't remember Lurene Tuttle from *Walking Tall*, you might remember seeing her as a lady shoplifter on "The Andy Griffith Show." I'm glad Mamaw never knew that the actress playing her had a criminal past on TV. She would have *really* disapproved then!)

Many fans of the film may not know it, but when *Walking Tall* opened in late February 1973, it appeared to be a flop after the first three weeks. It ran for only a couple of days at the theater in Selmer, and that must have been the pattern across the country.

Charles Pratt, the president of Bing Crosby Productions, called in the troops. He met with the folks of Cinerama Company, which was the distributor of the film, and they reevaluated the original promotional plan. It basically played up the violence, and, in retrospect, perhaps that kept a lot of families, especially parents with younger children, from going to see it.

Pratt and the others conceived a new promotion—this time based on the idea of a good man who bucked "the system" and who had a wife who was true blue. The posters were redone to reflect the decision.

The public-relations campaign also played up "the true story" angle, and in a new batch of newspaper advertisements and in television and radio commercials, the copy read, "Buford Pusser is a flesh and blood hero, one that can be touched, tell his own story, and sign autographs."

Unfortunately, the very same promotional scheme shied away from the truth as it said: "filmed on location in McNairy County, Tennessee, where it actually happened." Obviously, everybody in our hometown knew the movie wasn't filmed there, but not everybody knew why. Everyone back home also knew there was a lot of doctoring up of the true story, but that's Hollywood and that was also out of Daddy's control.

Despite any disappointments Daddy had about the movie, the new publicity plans went like gangbusters. *Walking Tall* went from the outhouse to become a box-office champ.

It churned up huge crowds across the United States. At one theater in Atlanta, it ran for thirty-nine weeks. At the drive-in theater in Savannah, it played for fourteen straight weeks, with sellouts every night. Daddy was on cloud nine.

It cost approximately one and a half-million dollars to make *Walking Tall*. The return was more than fifty million dollars. When *Photoplay* polled its readers, four million of them voted *Walking Tall* as Motion Picture of the Year.

While the movie was making Daddy famous, it was also opening the door to meeting the rich and famous. It was mostly the rich and famous wanting to meet him.

I mentioned earlier that fellow Tennessean Elvis Presley had met Daddy through their mutual friend Eddie Bond at Eddie's nightclub in Memphis. Some time after this, Daddy was flying back from Los Angeles on a commercial flight. The movie company evidently was paying for Daddy's flight, because he was riding up in first class.

He said that after he had boarded the plane and sat down, from two rows behind him he heard somebody holler, "Buford!" Daddy just sat there for a minute and said he thought to himself, "Somebody knows me."

He said he turned around and looked back, and when he did he could tell the person was in disguise. He turned back around and was thinking, "They're going to try to kill me here on this plane!" That's all he could think of.

"Are they going to do this before we take off?" he wondered. He was not familiar with the plane or the exit doors. He was thinking, "What am I going to do? We can't get these people hurt. What's going to happen?"

Then Daddy turned back around and the man said, "Buford!" Daddy got up and slowly went back to see what was up with this stranger sitting by the window.

Daddy leaned over the seat and asked, "Who in the hell are you?"

The disguised man said, "Buford, it's Elvis."

Daddy asked, "Elvis who?"

The man said, "How many people do you know from Tennessee who are named Buford and Elvis?"

Daddy said, "My gosh, you've scared me to death! I thought, 'Who in the world on this plane knows me?' I just

Daddy and Miss Tennessee 1973, Anne Galloway, met during a publicity appearance at E. B. Smith Chevrolet in Nashville in October 1973. They enjoyed a brief and proper courtship, and I still enjoy her friendship to this day.

knew you were somebody who was going to get up and try to do something to me."

Elvis said, "Sit down with me."

Daddy said no, but Elvis said, "No, I have both of these

seats. They're mine. I paid for both of these."

So Elvis and Daddy flew back together. After they got to Memphis, Daddy called home. We had phones everywhere in our house. I guess we had as many phones as the people at the telephone company. Every room had telephone jacks. The phone rang and Mamaw went to answer it, and I answered it in my bedroom.

I hollered, "Hey, Daddy! Hey, Daddy!" But I heard him say first to Mamaw, "Mother, I'm just going to stay in Memphis tonight. I rode back on the plane with Elvis, and I'm just going to go stay at Graceland."

Well, of course I went, "Ohhhmygosh! You're getting to stay at Graceland! Oh my goodness!"

And Daddy said, "Hush, Dwana, hush."

"Please get me an autograph! Please, Daddy, please!"

He said, "O.K., Dwana, I'll get you one."

Oh boy! I was so excited. Sure enough, the next day my daddy came in with a glossy photo that Elvis signed: *To Dwana . . . Love, Elvis Presley.* I keep it in a bank vault.

One time after this, Daddy pulled up to the house. I looked out the front door and called out, "Who's in the car with you?"

Daddy said, "Oh, that's Eddie Bond."

I knew Eddie, of course. I loved him to death. Daddy went inside to talk to my grandmother. I went out there and was talking to Eddie through the side window. There was also a man in the backseat. It was already dark outside, and I really couldn't see his face. I kind of looked at him, but nobody ever told me who he was. I'm sure I said hello or something to the other man and just kept talking to Eddie. I bounced back into the house, and Daddy got in the car and left.

The next morning, Daddy and Mamaw were talking about Elvis being in the car. And I said, "Elvis! Where was he?"

Daddy said, "Here. He was in the car last night."

"Why didn't you tell me?"

He said, "Because we didn't want the whole neighborhood

and town to know he was in there. That's why we didn't tell you, Dwana."

I couldn't believe that was who was in Daddy's back-seat. I would have paid a lot more attention to him, but to me the big star at that time was Eddie Bond. I mean, he had his own TV show on Channel 13 every Saturday, and from time to time we got to go be on it.

I had no idea the King was in the backseat of the car! So that was the first time I had actually seen him up close. I just didn't know I was seeing him because the car was dark. And it's not like you expect to see Elvis in the backseat of a car in your driveway. For all of those people who are still looking for Elvis, take it from me: don't forget to check the backseats of cars in your own driveway. You never can tell.

Let me share two other quick tales of Daddy's encounters with big stars.

At some point in the early 1970s, maybe 1973, singer-songwriter Jimmy Buffett had been recording one of his early albums in a Nashville studio. Things weren't going too well, so he and two of his pals left the studio and tied into a bottle of tequila. From there they drove to Roger Miller's King of the Road Hotel, where Buffett was staying. The trio, now feeling very well oiled, rode the elevator up to the Roof Club looking for some action, but the band was off that night. Jimmy and one of the pals, drummer Sammy Creason, then got onstage and began picking and singing. After running off most of the patrons, they decided to go out for some barbecue.

Buffett was wearing golf shoes that had had the cleats removed, but they still clicked as he walked. Once they got to the parking lot, he couldn't remember where he parked his car, a rented Gremlin. So Buffett climbed up on the hood of the first car he saw in order to get a better look around for his car. Well, lo and behold, that was my Daddy's car. He was in Nashville staying at the same hotel.

About that time, Daddy came outside and hollered at Buffett, telling him that he was under arrest. Buffett and

Creason scrambled for their Gremlin and jumped in, but not before Daddy closed in. Buffett had trouble starting the car, which gave Daddy time enough to reach in through the rolled-down passenger window past Creason, who was stabbing at Daddy's arm with a pen. Daddy grabbed a big handful of Buffett's hair and yanked it out.

They finally got the window up, but some say that by then Daddy had gotten a good grip on the Gremlin and, as he was rocking it, asked the duo, "Do you want me to turn this car over?"

Realizing that Daddy might be able to do just that, Buffett and his pal zoomed out of the parking lot pronto.

During this entire incident, Buffett had no idea who the big brute was that he had tangled with that day. After eating barbecue, the two realized they would have to return to the hotel to spend the night, so Buffett carried in the tire tool from the trunk of the Gremlin, just in case. They made it safely to their room on the eighth floor but then discovered they didn't have their room key. So Buffett went down to the front desk, the tire tool resting in his back pocket. While he was talking to the night clerk, Daddy came up from behind and pulled the tool out of his pocket.

He and Daddy got into a shouting match that was about to become violent. The bellman, who knew the music people and took pretty good care of them, dragged Buffett away to the elevator and got him back to the eighth floor, where he asked Buffett, "Do you know who that is?"

Buffett reportedly responded, "No, I don't."

When the bellman told him that it was Buford Pusser, Buffett decided it was definitely time to retire for the evening.

Another incident took place at the E. B. Smith Chevrolet car dealership in Nashville, where Burt Reynolds and Daddy were both signing autographs at the same time before a concert. A couple of women came running up to Burt and asked, "Where's that sheriff? We want his autograph."

Reynolds said, laughing, "He's right down there—that big ol' country bumpkin."

Reynolds then turned to Tammy Wynette, who was with him, and commented, "I can't believe they wanted to see him rather than me." Maybe it's just a coincidence that four years later in *Smokey and the Bandit*, Reynolds' archrival would be a bumbling sheriff named Buford, played by Jackie Gleason.

Daddy really worked hard plugging *Walking Tall*. He visited thirty-five states and five foreign countries. He must have signed thousands of autographs.

For all of the thrill and glamor and excitement associated with the movie, I'm sure Daddy would have traded away the movie and the fame and the money it brought to have been just a normal guy with a wife and kids. But our lives went on.

The movie probably cost him the election for sheriff in 1972. He was on the set of the film every day, but he was also campaigning during the filmmaking. A lot of folks were simply jealous of Daddy.

Juanita Richardson remembers the period, because it was after our house had burned, and Daddy and Mike were living at her motel.

"He lived here for four and a half months," Miss Juanita says. "Mike would go in and out between here and his grandparents' house. Buford was just elated over the movie. Mort Briskin stayed here too. They told him they weren't going to let him film in McNairy County.

"After the movie was made and everyone went berserk, then they wanted the other movies made here. I know that the county begged to have them made here, but the movie company said, 'No way.'"

Miss Juanita says she stood in a line "from here to yonder" when she went to Jackson to see *Walking Tall*. "We stood in line forever and we were there early, too. It was fairly accurate in a general way. When you get down to the nitty-gritty of it, it was true, but a lot of it was glamorized."

Miss Juanita will tell you about the day that Daddy got his

Daddy went to London in December 1973 to promote *Walking Tall*. Just as police officers across the United States were fans of my father, British peacekeepers and bobbies wanted to get close to the famous sheriff from Tennessee.

Daddy had lost his luggage at the airport, and therefore he didn't have a black-tie outfit to wear when he was invited to the house of Johnny Cash in Hendersonville, Tennessee, in November 1973. The Man in Black, Billy Graham (center), and a bunch of Nashville Republicans tried to talk Daddy into running for the office of governor.

first check from Bing Crosby Productions, for about ninety thousand dollars. He had a certain place where he always sat in the motel's restaurant—a round table in the corner where all the guys drank coffee and swapped tall tales.

Daddy told Miss Juanita's husband, Joe, "Go get Juanita." Then he held out that check and said, "Look! Look at those zeros!"

And then he put the check away because he didn't want to show everybody in there, but he was so proud. Miss Juanita and Joe were like family to him. He was just thrilled to death, and they were thrilled for him. He didn't go in there showing the check to everybody, but he wanted these two close friends to see what he'd received.

Losing the election hurt Daddy very much. The vote was 3,934 for incumbent Clifford Coleman and 3,251 for Daddy. He said of all the things he had lost in being sheriff, including

Dolly Parton and Daddy pose for the camera near Morristown in East Tennessee, where they were promoting a boat race.

his wife and the pain that was inflicted on him physically and mentally, he was still hurt very badly by that loss. He felt as though he had given up so much for the citizens, and it really hurt him down deep that they didn't return him to office. I believe he felt shunned, if not betrayed.

Although Daddy was knocked out of the local elections, he kept his hand in politics by helping to promote Ray Blanton, a friend and native of Adamsville who was a Democrat in the race for Tennessee governor. Daddy stumped in sixty Tennessee counties for Blanton over a three-week period that summer of 1974.

There are a lot of people who don't want other people to do well. I've never understood why some folks are like that. Maybe they thought that Daddy was becoming too successful from the movie—getting above his raising and that sort of thing. And I must say that instead of anything good that might have come from the movie, believe me, I would much rather have just had my mother and daddy at home.

A lot of people see *Walking Tall* and think it's really

Daddy is swarmed by fans as he appears at a car dealership. Many have brought copies of *The Twelfth of August* for him to sign. (Courtesy of *The Tennessean*)

Johnny Paycheck and I got to spend a little time together at the Adamsville Jaycees Buford Pusser Day on October 21, 1973. (Photograph by John George, *Memphis Press Scimitar,* courtesy of Mississippi Valley Collection, University of Memphis Libraries)

something—that it has a real significance. Compared to losing your family, it's nothing. On the other hand, as events in our family's life went, the movie was a peak. None of us imagined the terrible dark valley that awaited us after the bright lights from Hollywood had touched our lives.

CHAPTER 12

The Death of My Daddy

There was no doubt about it. Daddy loved a fast car.

McNairy County had over five hundred square miles that Daddy had to patrol. I think that was one of the attractions of law enforcement for him. He loved to drive fast in a souped-up car. If he were chasing bootleggers or some other lawbreakers, chances were good that they were driving a souped-up car, too. They weren't going to be in some family sedan just off the lot—that is, unless they had just stolen it.

Daddy also liked to trade cars. He had Thunderbirds,

Daddy stands beside his Corvette in the parking lot of the Old Home Restaurant in the spring of 1974. How did he ever pack his six-foot-six frame inside that little sports car?

Galaxies, and LTDs. After the ambush that killed my mother, trading cars also gave him an edge in both law enforcement and personal safety. About the time the criminals would become used to seeing him driving a certain car, he'd trade it in for a totally different car.

It seemed Daddy was more of a Ford man than a Chevrolet man. The last personal car that he purchased was a Lincoln Town Car. No matter what the car, they all had to have special high-performance engines. In October of 1973, he received a maroon 1974 Corvette from Gene Crump Chevrolet in Tuscumbia, Alabama, in exchange for his doing promotional projects for the dealership. Sure, it wasn't a Ford, but you don't look a gift Chevrolet in the mouth—especially if it's a Corvette.

When Mr. Crump asked Daddy what kind of car he wanted, Daddy replied with a grin, "Why, a Corvette, of course."

Mr. Crump was surprised. "Buford, do you think a great big man like you can even fit in a Corvette?"

"Oh yes, I think I'll fit in *juuust* nice," Daddy replied.

The Corvette also provided a chance for Daddy to give a little playful payback to Clifford Coleman, the current sheriff who beat Daddy in the 1972 race. Their relationship had become strained. Daddy ran into Coleman one night in 1973, not long after Daddy had gotten his new Corvette. Daddy insisted that Coleman get in the car because he wanted to show him how it ran. Coleman knew better than to ride with Daddy, but he also knew better than to argue with Daddy too much either. Off they went so fast that Coleman begged and pleaded for Daddy to slow down. Coleman later told how he had been through World War II and three terms as sheriff but had never been as scared in his life as he was that night. When he finally crawled out of the Corvette, he said he kissed the ground in thanks for still being alive.

Clifford Coleman wasn't the only one with safety concerns around that time. For a while, and especially since I had turned thirteen in January 1974, I had been especially nervous about something bad happening to Daddy. I guess it was partly because I knew that the number thirteen was supposed to be unlucky, but on another level, I was just worried because Daddy had been away a lot during the last year promoting the movie and making personal appearances. When Daddy wasn't around as much, I worried about his safety and mine. I was also going through the normal teenage anxieties and was butting heads constantly with Mamaw—probably because there was such a generation gap between us and also she was often the only one around to butt heads with.

My nerves got so bad in the spring of 1974 that my pediatrician, Dr. Ross Smith, decided that the best thing was to put me in the hospital for a few days just to calm me down. Dr. Smith quickly determined the root of my problem. He told Daddy, "Buford, what this child needs is her father. She's already lost her mother. Now, she's worried sick that she's going to lose you. She needs to spend more time with you."

Daddy went home and coincidentally got pretty much the same stern advice from our longtime neighbor, Norma Woods, who had become like a mother to me and still is. With those double-barreled shots of parenting wisdom, Daddy immediately took steps to spend more time with me. He and Dr. Smith made arrangements with my school principal, T. E. Chisholm, the same man who had been one of Daddy's high-school coaches, to allow me to have Thursdays and Fridays off from school in order to spend more time with Daddy. This way I could spend four-day weekends with Daddy and accompany him to his personal appearances or just enjoy father-daughter activities.

This time together meant so much to me. It was just what the doctor—and Norma Woods—had ordered. And it was just what I needed to help heal and turn the tide on what I'm sure must have been some serious emotional issues brewing in me. I still worried, but being around my daddy soothed much of my anxiety.

Daddy did several promotional tours that summer. He even flew out to Bing Crosby Productions in Hollywood at

There was a big parade down Main Street in Adamsville on the Saturday morning of Buford Pusser Day Weekend in October 1973. I thought I was really dressed up for the shindig as Daddy met with lots of his admirers and signed dozens of autographs.

the end of July to do a movie screen test for the *Walking Tall* sequel. Even so, he still made sure that there was time to take me on a trip to Disney World. It was a trip I will never forget. I was so excited. I got to take my friend Tina from next door with me. As soon as we got into the airport in Memphis and again in Orlando, everybody recognized Daddy. It was as if he were a movie star. And I guess, in a way, he was.

That trip was so incredibly good for me because I needed that precious time with my daddy. We rode all the rides and saw all the shows that Disney World had to offer. For four days, he was just my daddy. I remember that we waited in line for a really long time for one particular show. When we finally wound our way back and forth through the line and got into the show, Daddy said, "I can't believe that I've just stood in line for an hour and fifteen minutes to watch a bunch of bears dance." Maybe he would have liked the bears better if he'd been allowed to wrestle them.

Even if Daddy didn't go for the dancing bears, those four days were among the most wonderful of my young life. I am so grateful for those memories. After we flew home, Daddy found out that the movie producers had decided he could make the grade as an actor. He really was going to be a movie star now!

On the morning of Tuesday, August 20, 1974, shortly after we had returned from Florida, a press conference was held at the Rivermont Hotel in Memphis. CBS, ABC, NBC, and the wire services covered the press conference as it was announced that Daddy was going to portray himself in *Buford,* the sequel to *Walking Tall.* He was also going to help write the script. In a few days, the Crosby people were planning to scout locations around the area with Daddy.

After the press conference, Daddy came on back home. He was driving his Lincoln Town Car because his Corvette was at Maxedon's Phillips 66 station having some work done. The sports car had been having some minor motor problems. He stopped off at the service station on the way home to check on his Corvette and pay for the work. He made arrangements to have the car delivered to our house. He then left to run a few other errands. He stopped off to

This was one of the last photographs made of Daddy. It was taken in Memphis the morning he announced he would star as himself in the film *Buford*. He died just before midnight that same day. (Photograph by Richard Gardner, *Memphis Commercial Appeal*, courtesy of Mississippi Valley Collection, University of Memphis Libraries)

share his news from the press conference with friends at the Old Home Restaurant.

Sometime that afternoon, he ran into Miss Flora Pyron, whom Daddy had known ever since he and his parents had moved to Adamsville. When he was a teenager, Daddy used to cut through her yard on the way to and from school. He spent many an afternoon visiting on her front porch. A lot of times, she would have milk and cookies for him to snack on when he came by.

On this particular day, Daddy ran into Miss Flora in back of Walker's grocery as she was about to go inside. She asked Daddy if she could borrow twenty dollars until the end of the month. She said she had had a lot of medical bills and such that month and things were a little tighter than usual. Daddy already knew she was on a fixed income.

Miss Flora later told me how Daddy reached into his billfold and pulled out a $100 bill. He said, "Here, Miss Flora, you don't owe this back to me. I want to give this to you because of all the times I came to your house and you fed me and you saw to me. You don't owe me a thing. You take this and buy whatever you need."

Miss Flora went and shopped for what she needed. When she got to the checkout, Mr. Walker was expecting her to put her items on credit, but she gave him the $100 bill. Mr. Walker asked her, "Why, Miss Flora, where in the world did you get this?"

She told him how Daddy had given her the money. Mr. Walker later said that for some reason, he had taken that $100 bill, written *Buford Pusser* on it, and stuck it in his billfold.

After dropping by various places to chew the fat with a few more friends, Daddy headed home. Being just a regular guy, he put on a pair of shorts and a T-shirt and mowed the yard that afternoon. During that time, the Corvette was delivered by two men who worked at the station. Daddy was very particular about his cars, so he took it out for a road test. Everything must have checked out fine because he didn't send it back to the station for any additional work. After he finished mowing,

Mr. O. R. Walker displays the $100 bill that Daddy gave to Miss Flora Pyron on the last afternoon of his life. (Photograph by John George, *Memphis Press Scimitar,* courtesy of Mississippi Valley Collection, University of Memphis Libraries)

he washed the Corvette, got cleaned up, and drove the Corvette over to Wolf Brothers Restaurant in Savannah, Tennessee, to visit with old friends and have supper.

After leaving the restaurant, he drove to Selmer to meet

Daddy sits behind the wheel of his Corvette as a Bible, a gun, and a badge lie on the dashboard.

my friend Tina and me at the McNairy County Fair and Livestock Show at around nine o'clock. It was his custom to attend the fair because he was usually recruited to sit in the dunking booth to help raise money for the Jaycees. There were always a lot of people who wanted to take a shot at Daddy, but at least in this case it was for a good cause.

The same fair had been coming to town for a long time, and everybody knew my daddy—from the carnies and the farmers to the school kids and the businesspeople. Even though he was larger than life, here he was just regular old Buford to them.

Still, there was a lot of excitement around him that night. I remember how every time we went by a food booth, the vendor would ask Daddy, "Here, you want a cotton candy?" or "Have a candy apple" or "How about the girls? Do they want corndogs? Popcorn? A cold drink?" I would stand there and think, "Oh, I wish they'd all just shut up and quit talking to him." I wanted him to myself.

It was a hot, humid night—the muggy kind of night that just sort of sticks to you and is so typical of West Tennessee in August. A quick dip in the dunking booth probably would have felt pretty good, but Daddy never got in the dunking booth that night. Either the machine broke or maybe he simply hadn't been scheduled because he had been out of town so much. Instead of getting a refreshing dunk, he just continued to walk around the midway with us. As we strolled past the various skill games, he stopped to play several of them, such as shooting a basketball into a hoop, throwing a football through a tire swing, and tossing a plastic ring around the neck of a bottle.

He won three teddy bears and two dolls for Tina and me that night. Even the most expertly rigged carnival game was no match for Daddy's dead aim and delicate touch. Anything he won, he earned. The prizes weren't just given to us because of who he was. Daddy wouldn't allow that. He had to actually win everything. He didn't want people giving me things just because I was his daughter. Maybe it was the competitive streak in him, too.

We just had an all-around good time that night. But all good things must end.

We were getting ready to leave and everyone was talking to Daddy and visiting with him. Tina's mother was supposed to be there to pick up Tina and me around eleven o'clock, but she wasn't there yet. We kept waiting at the gate, and Daddy waited with us. We waited until about 11:40, when Daddy finally told the guy at the gate that Tina's mom would be driving a green Monte Carlo and that he should tell her that we had gone home with him.

As we started toward Daddy's Corvette, a man stopped us and detained us. I truly believe today that he was some sort of lookout. I don't believe it just happened. He talked to Daddy just long enough for Tina's mom and a friend, Jason Hollingsworth, to arrive. So, Tina and I got in the car with them. I said goodbye to Daddy and "I love you." We headed for home, which was just over ten miles back down Highway 64. We couldn't have been gone for more than just a couple of minutes when Daddy came up behind us and then passed us, which was nothing unusual to me because he was known for driving fast. He was a good driver and he was used to driving at very high speeds.

As he sped past us, Tina's mother said, "Buford had better slow down or he'll get killed before he gets home," and I said, "Oh no, Miss Shirley, please don't say that, please don't say that."

As we drove down Highway 64, we came to a curve near the community of Lawton. As we made our way around this curve, we could see an embankment in the distance that was visible at night because of a light post and a little store

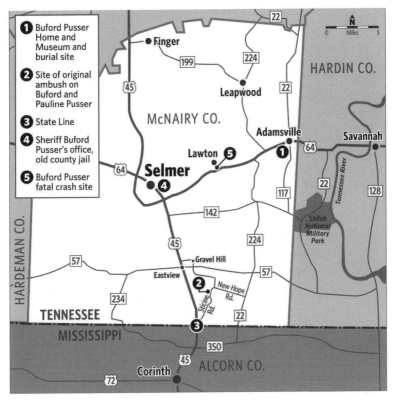

that were in that area. We could see something had happened as we went down the hill.

I shouted, "Oh my gosh, it's a wreck! Oh my gosh, it's my daddy! It's my daddy! I just know it's my daddy!" After we stopped at the scene, I jumped out of the car and ran over to where Daddy was lying face down behind the Corvette. The front end of the car was on fire.

I turned him over and began screaming, "Daddy! Daddy! Daddy! Daddy, don't die! Daddy, don't die!" He muttered what I want to think was "Dwana," and then he was gone. I knew that he was dead. I had lost my daddy. I had lost my best friend.

I started screaming, "Somebody help me! Help me move him!" I wanted to move him away because he was so close to the burning car. I was not going to allow his body to burn.

There were two men standing near us at the scene as I cried for help, but they didn't want to get involved. As I was only thirteen, it had to have been the adrenaline flowing through my body, and the fear—I didn't want him to burn behind that car. Without even stopping to think about how impossible it was, I lifted my daddy up.

I don't know how, but I carried him a good fifty feet from the car.

Sometime later, shortly after midnight, Daddy would be officially pronounced dead at the scene by Dr. Harry Peeler, the McNairy County medical examiner. The medical cause of death would be ruled a broken neck. I didn't need to wait for the official word.

The T-top was off of the Corvette that night. The police report said Daddy was thrown from the vehicle, but there are a number of things in the report that to this day I'm not sure about.

I didn't know it at the time, but a man named Danny Browder, who lived in a nearby trailer and happened to have graduated from high school with Daddy, had heard the wreck while watching a late-night movie on TV. The noise caused him to think it was a jet plane that had crashed. He immediately went outside, got in his car, and backed it up. As he turned his car east, his headlights hit Daddy's car approximately two hundred feet away.

Without recognizing whose car it was, Browder knew the seriousness of what had happened, went back inside his home, and called for the police. By the time he drove back down to the scene, I was already there. Shortly afterward, Adamsville policeman T. W. Burks and highway patrolman Paul Ervin of Selmer arrived, and we were forced to move behind his patrol car because the fire was igniting the bullets that Daddy always kept in his car.

When they calmed me down, my neighbors and a city policeman took me home. As we entered the house, I said to my grandmother, "Mamaw, Daddy's had a wreck and he's dead."

My grandmother was so shocked that she slapped my jaw and commanded, "Don't you ever, ever say that again!"

I cried out again, "Mamaw, he's dead!"

She grabbed me by the arm, and she wouldn't believe me until she got on the telephone and called the local funeral home, whose ambulance had gone to retrieve Daddy's body. She was in shock.

Later, I found out one of the reasons why my grandmother was in such a state.

Daddy had told us two weeks before his death that a contract had been put out on his life. He thought it might be because he had agreed to support Ray Blanton for governor. But there was a little more to it.

Ray Blanton was from Adamsville. He was a congressman and his father had been mayor of Adamsville. He was a Democrat and Daddy was a Republican. They knew each other but were never what you would call close friends. Be that as it may, an influential group of local matriarchs, including Ray's mother, had sat Daddy down one day and basically said, "Now, Buford, you've just got to support Ray for governor. It's not going to look good if he doesn't have your support in his own hometown."

Daddy said, "Well, you go back and tell Ray that the only way I'll back him is if he'll make me Commissioner of Safety if he's elected." The matriarchs made the deal.

Daddy knew that in such a key position, he could open up a lot of old cases and obtain warrants that might otherwise have been prevented by people in high places. There were a lot of people who wouldn't have wanted him to be in that powerful of a position.

The day of my father's wreck, my grandmother had been getting phone calls from a man who wanted to talk to Daddy. I didn't know about these calls until a few days later.

"I need to talk to Buford," the caller kept telling her.

She said, "Well, Buford is mowing the grass." Then he called back and she replied, "He's just left to get something to eat." And then he called back and she said, "He's gone to the fair."

The caller told her, "I have to get word to him. They are going to try to kill him tonight."

My grandmother didn't know the nature of the calls until it was too late. When I came in that night and told her what had happened, I think it was her shock and her guilt that must have hit her. It was very hard to convince her that her son was really dead.

Losing a parent is hard for anybody. The pain of losing a parent a second time is almost indescribable—especially when you feel as close as I felt to Daddy. He was my whole world. He was my daddy. He was my mother. He was my buddy.

When I had turned thirteen earlier in the year, I had been superstitiously afraid that something bad was going to happen to Daddy. Even after I became more calm with my "nerve treatment," I still prayed each night when I would go to bed: "Dear Lord, please just take care of my daddy and please don't let him die. I need him so bad. I need him so bad."

I was scared to death about what was going to happen to us now. All my worries were coming true. I had lost my mother when I was six, and I had thought, "How could such a horrible thing happen?" And now I thought, "How in the world could the Lord take my daddy from me, too?" I was in shock—completely and utterly traumatized—lost.

I look at things differently now than I looked at them then. I just have to know that this must have been what God had in His plans.

With that said, I don't think my father's death was an accident. I believe he was murdered.

On that stretch of road, there really wasn't that much of a curve, and he had driven it so many times. It was a clear night and the car should have been in excellent condition—especially after the mechanical work that had just been done.

I know accidents happen, but I cannot believe, even if he'd been going 120 miles per hour, that he would have lost control. I think he could have driven through that stretch with his eyes closed.

There was speculation after his death that maybe he didn't know how to drive that Corvette since it was the current 1974 model and seemed as if it was brand new. The fact is that Daddy had had that Corvette for almost a year. He knew that car inside and out and had already logged many miles in it.

There was another car that rolled by the scene shortly after the wreck and before the police arrived. Some have speculated that Daddy and the other driver had been in some sort of spur-of-the-moment drag race and that Daddy had simply lost control. But there was no hard evidence at the wreck site to support the racing theory. However, there was a second set of fresh tire tracks that might have indicated another kind of involvement with a second vehicle.

Others speculate that the Corvette was tampered with—specifically that the tie rods had been cut, which, if they had come completely apart, would have caused the car to be impossible to steer. Any evidence pointing in that direction was hastily dismissed by the primary McNairy County investigators. Even though several people thought there were indications of tampering, the tie rods and other physical evidence were destroyed immediately after the "investigation."

Hundreds of curiosity seekers came to check out the scene on the highway between Selmer and Adamsville where Daddy's Corvette crashed and burned. Here, two people look over the burned-out hulk of the car. (Photograph by William Leaptrott, *Memphis Press Scimitar*, courtesy of Mississippi Valley Collection, University of Memphis Libraries)

Two weeks after the wreck, my daddy's death was ruled an accident by the official investigators.

I always had my doubts about that conclusion. Everything didn't add up. There were a lot of unanswered questions that the brief investigation never pursued. Pieces of the puzzle were missing. It wouldn't be until 1990, sixteen years after Daddy's death, that I would receive a document that I knew could be a giant missing piece of the puzzle. It reinforced my worst suspicions. It would be another fifteen years—and more than thirty years after the wreck—before I got to the point where I felt that I could deal with the consequences of revealing the contents of that document and how they support my suspicions about the cause of the wreck.

As for the last minutes of August 20 and early moments of August 21, 1974, there's no doubt about one thing. Daddy loved a fast car. And that is how he died.

CHAPTER 13

Daddy's Funeral

Some time in the early hours of Wednesday morning, the ambulance carried Daddy's body to McNairy County General Hospital. He had been pronounced dead at the scene of the accident by Dr. Peeler. A few hours later, Daddy's remains were transported to Shackelford Funeral Home in Selmer, where he had briefly worked as an ambulance driver after he graduated from high school.

On Thursday, Daddy's body was moved to Shackelford Funeral Home in Adamsville. We knew that throngs of people would be coming to pay their last respects, so the family decided to have his body lie in state at the Adamsville Church of Christ for forty-eight hours before the funeral.

Daddy had a bulldog named Little Bull that lay down and cried and mourned the whole time Daddy's body lay in state. Little Bull hardly ate after Daddy died. Thirty days later, he died in his doghouse. He was thirteen years old, just like me.

At two o'clock that Thursday afternoon, Daddy's body was transported to the church. This was the same sanctuary where we had the funeral service for my mother almost exactly seven years earlier.

The flowers poured in from people from around the world, even from fans as far away as Australia. Wreaths and floral arrangements were everywhere in the church. Someone counted them at nearly two hundred. Floral arrangements lined the hallways and stacked up four deep behind the podium. On the side of the sanctuary were baskets and baskets of flowers. The flowers came from friends, police forces, state officials, and high-school football teams across the state.

Lying on the $6,000 coffin was a wreath of red roses with a green sash that read *Daddy*. Ray Blanton, for whom Daddy had been campaigning in the race for governor, had sent a large floral arrangement shaped like a book, with the title *Walking Tall* on the cover. George Jones and Tammy Wynette sent a four-foot white chrysanthemum arrangement shaped like a guitar and lined with red. Tanya Tucker also sent flowers.

Our family had requested that, in lieu of flowers, donations be made to Adamsville City Park. This was later renamed Buford Pusser Memorial Park, because Daddy had a special place in his heart for the kids in town and he had wanted them to have a nice place to play.

Daddy had told me that he was going to build a swimming pool the next time he got a royalty check from the movie company. I got so excited. I asked him where in our yard he planned to put it. He said, "It's not going to be in our yard. I'm going to put it across the street in the city park so all the kids can have a place to swim." I'm so pleased that funds were donated in his memory for that park.

Our little town swelled to overflowing in the days leading up to the funeral. More than three thousand people walked past Daddy's casket. On Saturday, the day of the funeral, the Old Home Restaurant, one of Daddy's favorite places, was forced to close at noon because they just couldn't handle the masses of people.

Besides the public, politicians, and policemen, there were several celebrities who came to say goodbye to Daddy. He had made a number of friends in country music.

Joe Don Baker and Daddy had become very good friends during the filming of *Walking Tall*. Joe Don had spent the night at our house. When Daddy had been to California, he

Daddy's funeral procession travels down Main Street of Adamsville, where hundreds of people stand and pay their final respects to Tennessee's most famous lawman. (Photograph by Dave Darnell, *Memphis Commercial Appeal,* courtesy of Mississippi Valley Collection, University of Memphis Libraries)

had spent the night at Joe Don's house. When Joe Don made the movie *Framed* in Nashville earlier in 1974, he and Daddy had done some honky-tonking together.

Joe Don, who served as an honorary pallbearer, told the press, "I guess some people could say I'm here to make myself look good. I'm here because I love him. He was a hero to me."

Perhaps the biggest surprise was when we got a phone call from the president of the United States, Richard Nixon, expressing his condolences. Actually, the White House called three times before my grandmother talked with President Nixon, because our neighbor Miss Norma kept hanging up. She thought they were crank calls. Adamsville police chief James Robertson, who already had his hands full providing security for the funeral, had to drop what he was doing to come by our house and tell us to quit hanging up on the White House.

In the hour or so before the funeral, the celebrities were gathered in the backroom of the house in what had been my brother Mike's bedroom. In that room were Joe Don Baker and his wife, George Jones and Tammy Wynette, and a man in the corner whom I finally recognized as Elvis Presley. He had on black pants, a gray turtleneck, a black jacket, and sunglasses. He put his arm around me and told me how sorry he was. I remember him telling me, "I'm so sorry. I'm so sorry, little darling." And he hugged me.

The men handling security had snuck Elvis and the others into the back bedroom because there were a lot of people in the other end of the house, and the security people wanted to be able to bring the celebrities in and out quickly. Fortunately, our house had all of those extra doors from when Daddy rebuilt it after the fire and wanted to make sure everyone could easily get to an exit from anywhere in the house.

The security men escorted the celebrities out the back door of the house and sat them in the side area of the church, where there was a set of folding doors. From that vantage point, the doors could be folded back to allow these people to observe from the side but without other people being able to get to them.

I'll always remember those special friends who came. One of them was Anne Galloway, Miss Tennessee of 1973, whom Daddy had dated and whom I liked very much.

During the service, uniformed policemen, state troopers, and sheriff's deputies stood in line along the aisles. Besides Tennessee, the officers hailed from nearby states, such as Alabama and Mississippi, and from as far away as Arizona.

Daddy was dressed for burial in a black suit with red and gray pinstripes. He had on a white shirt and a blue and red polka-dot tie. Even in death, Daddy was a sharp dresser.

Because the church building seated only 300 and there were so many people who wanted to hear the eulogy, special speakers were set up outside the building so folks out there could listen. Hundreds and hundreds of people stood in the churchyard. There were even adults up in the trees.

The funeral began at two o'clock. Much of the service is

Here I am with country-music legends Tammy Wynette and George Jones. How excited I was to meet them before they performed in our town. They returned for Daddy's funeral. Over the next several years, they invited me to their home numerous times.

Daddy, Anne Galloway (Miss Tennessee 1973), and I have front-row seats for the community worship service during the Buford Pusser Day Weekend in Adamsville on October 21, 1973.

blanked out in my mind. I remember scenes but not a lot of the details. Newspapers from across the state covered this second black day of my young life and reported on what was said.

Bobby Tillman, the minister of the Church of Christ, who also helped conduct my mother's funeral, read scriptures from the Bible and led a prayer. Among the songs sung were "Hold to God's Unchanging Hand," "Rock of Ages," and "The Last Mile of the Way."

The eulogy was delivered by the Reverend Russell Gallimore, formerly pastor of the United Methodist Church

Anne Galloway and I enjoyed the country-music show on Buford Pusser Day Weekend together. The performers included Tammy Wynette, George Jones, Johnny Paycheck, and Lynn Anderson. Daddy was a big fan of country music, and lots of Nashville's country singers were fans of Daddy.

in Adamsville, but who at the time of the funeral served the Bolivar Methodist Church.

The eulogy was brief, but the reverend compared Daddy

Carl Pusser, my grandfather, and Daddy's uncle Lloyd Harris make their way into the church for Daddy's funeral. Actor Joe Don Baker is just a few paces behind them. (Photograph by Dave Darnell, *Memphis Commercial Appeal,* courtesy of Mississippi Valley Collection, University of Memphis Libraries)

to another man who "walked tall," who saw oppression, injustice, and social sin and felt compelled to change it—"a man named Jesus Christ."

Jesus felt a "keen sense of righteousness within—not understanding why he felt it," the reverend said. "He sensed that some people might not understand what he did. Some might even think he was crazy. He figured he might lose some friends along the way."

In a place where force and brutality had been accepted, Jesus "saw a new day in which men could put aside guns and knives," the reverend said. "He took for his weapon a stick—a stick that was used against him—and in the final analysis, it took the form of a cross. Sadly, many rejoiced."

He added, "Jesus walked tall upon this earth long ago, so that every now and then another man comes along who chooses to walk tall today. It took a real man to make the devil run. He saw sins and vices and this struck a responsive chord. His vision was clean and strong and he steadfastly went about righting the wrongs."

Finally, he asked for divine comfort, saying that it would take "the Christ who walks tall on this earth to help us pass through this valley of grief."

I would be reminded of Daddy's quiet connection to this church in the months ahead and in a very touching way. One Sunday during the service, Deacon Henry Carruthers told the congregation that they may have noticed that the church's treasury, while never exactly overflowing, didn't seem quite as healthy as it had in the many months before. He explained that the reason was that my daddy had quietly been giving $100 a week for some time, in order to help pay off some of the debts incurred when the congregation constructed its new church building. Daddy had requested that his giving to the church in this way not be made public.

After Daddy died and that steady source of funds for the church was no longer coming in, Brother Carruthers felt obliged to the congregation and to my daddy's memory to explain the situation. It was the first I had heard about it. I found out later that, after the movie money had started coming in, Daddy had told Mamaw to write a $100 check to the church every week as long as we had enough money in the bank account to do so.

Daddy's final ride was in a gray hearse. The casket was light blue and covered in roses. It was a short procession for the vehicles as it was just a few blocks from the church to the cemetery where Daddy was laid to rest next to my mother.

Among the six pallbearers was Ray Blanton, who was soon to become governor of the state.

Approximately two hundred people attended the graveside ceremony. The reverend spoke a few more words, saying, "Buford's scarred body will return to dust, but his spirit will live on."

Officer Steve Hood, president of the Fraternal Order of Police of Shelby County, spoke briefly over the grave. Law-enforcement officers walked by the casket and each man put a white carnation on the lid.

The preacher read Matthew 14:12, and that was the end of it. The inscription on my mother and daddy's tombstone reads:

> Buford Pusser
> His wife
> Pauline
> Sheriff of McNairy
> County Tennessee
> 1964-1970
> He Walked Tall

I guess that says it all.

The final resting place of my mother and father. (Courtesy of Mississippi Valley Collection, University of Memphis Libraries)

Throughout these three days of painful grieving, more than anybody, my aunt Gailya and Miss Norma Woods from next door comforted me, took care of me, and helped me try to make sense of everything that had happened.

Miss Norma had done so much for me. One of my very favorite things was her lemon icebox pie. It was a real comfort food to me. Miss Norma made one of her pies and brought it over to our house for me during this time. When I came back from the funeral, there were people everywhere in the house. I went to the refrigerator to get some of my lemon icebox pie, and it was gone. I found out that Floyd Joyer with the movie company had gotten a hold of that pie and had eaten every bit of it. He had started in on the pie the night before and then the next day had finished it off. From then on, by association, I was mad at all of the movie people, because I kept thinking, "He ate my pie! The day of the funeral!" I know that was silly and childish, but then again, I was only thirteen.

But missing pies were a trifle. I was more concerned that I was going to be an orphan, because back when Mother had died, somebody had told my brother that he and I were going to be orphans. Now that Daddy was gone, I really believed that. I thought that I would probably be put in a state home. It scared me a lot.

Miss Norma and Aunt Gailya calmed me down and said, "No, you're not. You'll get help. You'll be all right." But that was still something that worried me more than anything.

When I look back, it amazes me that I did not lose my faith in the Lord. So many people don't understand that, and sometimes I don't. I think it has to be your leap of faith and your trust in the Lord, and do I believe in Him. I don't believe He causes bad things to happen, but He must have been there with me during the terrible time or I wouldn't be as sane as I am now—however sane that might be.

Still, I was totally fearful that I would be taken from my grandmother, that I was going to be an orphan and separated from my family, and that I would not be allowed to continue living in my own house.

My brother was married by this time. I guess I was think-ing, "If my sister is gone and my brother is gone, I am all by myself." I was scared of that thought.

I wondered how we would make ends meet—how we were going to make a living and have the money to go on. That really bothered me and not for foolish reasons. I was just afraid of how we would live without somebody being there to bring home a check.

When Mother was killed, my grandmother had come to live in our house and my grandfather stayed in their house or at the jail. I think that if she hadn't been a strong Christian, Mamaw would have gotten a divorce. My grand-mother put up with a lot of rambunctious behavior by my grandfather. Papaw would take a little nip of this and that. I never recall his going to church with us. I'm sure that was a source of worry for Mamaw.

I remember one time when I was little I tried to get Papaw to kiss my grandmother. It was Mamaw's birthday and I said, "Just kiss her, just kiss her." I remember begging for twen-ty minutes and he never would. I said, "Papaw, just go give her peck." Mamaw just stood there and stood there. Neither one would do anything.

My grandmother and I had a large generation gap. Maybe we were too much alike. I respect her so much now, and I regret being the ugly, smart-alecky kid that I was from time to time.

So there I was at thirteen. It was to be just Mamaw and me fending for ourselves. That probably could have and should have worked out a lot better than it did. Unfortunately, my father's estate was to become a big mess. Daddy left no will. On top of that, my grandmother made some decisions that brought a stranger to live in our house. Her actions ultimately only extended a nightmare that seemed as though it would never end.

CHAPTER 14

Picking Up the Pieces:
My Life Without Daddy

School started back a couple of weeks after my daddy's death. As it had been after my mother's murder almost seven years earlier, it was extremely difficult to get my mind and emotions under control starting the new year at school so soon after the death of my daddy.

Being a new teenager, with all of the typical anxieties and confusion that can occur at that age, I probably would have had a tough enough time handling the eighth grade anyway. During all of my years in school, I had had to cope with an extra measure of teasing because my daddy was the sheriff. There wasn't any teasing starting the eighth grade. Somehow that absence of what I had come to expect when at school, as annoying as it was, just drove home the sadness of losing my daddy all the more.

Not long after Daddy was killed, kids in our neighborhood decided to put on a backyard circus at one of their houses. Everyone in town was invited. We charged a small admission. When it was over, my friends surprised me by giving me all of the proceeds because of what had happened to me. That touched my heart so much.

Though I had always had friends to play with around the neighborhood, I rarely had anyone sleep over at my house when I was growing up. My friends' parents were scared for them to do so, because of Daddy's being sheriff and all of the violent and dangerous things that happened in his life. As a parent now myself, I understand that.

I was more worried than ever that now something might happen to my grandmother. She was really all that I had left in my life at home. Mike had gotten married the previous March and was no longer living at our home, though he was still in the area at that time. Diane had moved away from Adamsville. Papaw still lived in the house on Baptist Street, but he never moved into the house with my grandmother and me. He was just more comfortable at his own home. Mamaw would divide her time between the family needs at the two homes, but she basically lived fulltime at the house with me. However, we still spent a lot of time at Papaw's house and ate a lot of our meals there with him. We stayed there some, too.

In the eighth grade and earlier, I wanted so badly to be a basketball player, but I was always heavy growing up. I was afraid that there wouldn't be a basketball uniform to fit me. But I knew that the cheerleading outfits were custom made

My grandparents and I grin away for the camera while sitting in back of our house. (Courtesy of *The Tennessean*)

for each cheerleader. So in the eighth grade, I tried out for cheerleader and won. I was so excited. I was also a cheerleader in ninth and tenth grade. I'm sure my interest in being around sports was because my father had been very involved with sports. I had also watched Mike as he pursued his love of football and especially basketball. Diane had been a cheerleader. Sports were a family tradition.

I didn't think about it at the time, but looking back now I suppose it's ironic that, on the heels of all the family tragedy I had experienced, I would seek out an activity where I was leading cheers. I guess it buoyed me just to be involved in something that could take my mind off sad thoughts.

When I was growing up, I knew enough to start developing career ideas. From a fairly early age, I had thought I wanted to be a lawyer. I imagine that Daddy's involvement in law enforcement was a key reason for that interest. I saw that lawyers could help people with problems but did not have to face the daily dangers that policemen do. Worrying about my daddy and my family all my life made being a cop too scary for my nerves and dreams. Some things that happened after Daddy's death made a career in law even more appealing to me. If I could help other people, especially children, avoid being taken advantage of and swindled, then being a child advocate seemed to me like a worthwhile career.

Becoming a child psychologist was another career that appealed to me—again as a way to help children who had been through tragedies similar to what I had experienced. Then again, I think I always recognized that I was having enough trouble trying to keep my own mind together without trying to tackle other people's problems too.

It's not that I sought trouble. It's just that sometimes trouble comes knocking at your door without you ever having to go look for it.

I remember the very first day I saw Larry Britt. It was a bright, sunshiny day when he knocked at our front door. His brand-new, black Chrysler Cordoba was parked in the driveway. He said, "I'm here to see Mrs. Pusser. I'm a private investigator and I'm here to help her. She asked me to come here to see her."

My grandmother had become so immersed in trying to find out who had killed my daddy that she couldn't see what an awful conman Larry Britt was. I saw through him immediately, and my grandmother ordinarily would have, too. He had called her when he heard about my father's death. He saw a classic opportunity to prey on the emotions of a grieving mother and family. After much persuasion, he convinced my grandmother that he could investigate and eventually prove that her son was murdered. That played right into what she desperately wanted to believe.

Britt, his wife, stepson, and stepdaughter eventually wormed their way into our lives to the point that they were actually living with us. I may have been wishing that it wasn't just Mamaw and me living at our house, but having the Britt clan descending upon us definitely wasn't what I had in mind.

Prior to his a career as a "private investigator," Britt had been a funeral-home assistant in Wisconsin and car salesman in North Carolina. Through all of his years of "investigating" my father's death, all Larry Britt ever found was a way to go from having one Chrysler Cordoba to having two Lincoln Mark IVs. It was also strange that many of the leads he wanted to follow required him—and his wife—to take lengthy trips to Las Vegas. He tried to sound noble by declaring that he would charge us only for his living expenses. Of course, when your expenses include staying at Caesar's Palace and wining and dining all over Las Vegas for two months as you search for clues, then expenses can become expensive.

In 1976, my grandmother tried to have Daddy's body exhumed because Larry Britt had convinced her that Daddy had been poisoned. The courts refused to allow it, and Dr. Peeler, the county medical examiner, saw no need for it, but their refusal very much upset my grandmother.

What started my grandmother's interest in that angle was that a boy had reported that he saw somebody drop something in Daddy's beverage cup as he was about to leave the fairgrounds the night he died. Even at the time, I wondered if Larry Britt hadn't put the young man up to making that accusation. In the past few years, that same so-called witness has written me from prison in California and said that if I ever want to know what happened that night, I should write him and he would tell me. I've not written him back because I think he's just a con trying to pull a con.

One Christmas, the Britts celebrated the holidays at our house and brought my grandmother and me two little gifts that were paid for with the money my grandmother had paid Britt for "investigating." They then proceeded to open all of these extravagant presents that they had gotten for each other—once again paid for with our money—right before our eyes.

Britt made my grandmother believe that he was onto the story about how my daddy was killed. She so badly wanted to believe that her son was murdered and not just killed in a senseless accident that she was willing to continue investing thousands of dollars in that hope. She was such a savvy woman about business and other dealings. She was the last person any of us would have expected to fall for such an obvious conman. But investigating my father's death was her blind spot. Larry Britt, con artist that he was, exploited that weakness until there was nothing left to take.

Britt completely disrupted our lives. My grandmother became completely engrossed by his theories. He destroyed whatever life I had living with my grandmother.

My grandmother became so entangled in Larry Britt's web of lies and schemes that it became obvious to the court that my finances were in serious jeopardy. The court eventually had to take over guardianship of my finances. By that time, Britt had most of grandmother's money and more than a hundred thousand dollars of mine. I don't blame my grandmother. She was blinded by her grief and her obsession with the theory that someone had killed my father. She was also a proud person. She and I had fight after fight about Larry Britt during my teenage years.

In 1977 court proceedings, Britt testified that two movie executives and Lloyd Tatum—who was thought by many to be the sharpest lawyer around, which is why Daddy had hired him—conspired to have Daddy murdered. The very idea of that plot always seemed to me to be just plain nutty. What was truly alarming was that the court heard evidence that my portion of Daddy's estate shrank from more than $300,000 to a paltry $8,000. The court stepped in and issued a judgment ordering Aetna Insurance to pay $150,000 into my estate, because Aetna had insured Mamaw for $300,000 as guardian of the estate fund. Aetna must have successfully appealed that judgment, because I never received that money.

When the dust settled, there was still $60,000 unaccounted for at the time of my father's death. It became known that $40,000 of it was a loan to Ray Blanton, whom Daddy had supported for governor. The loan involved some Blanton property as collateral. The story went around that Blanton, Lloyd Tatum, and Daddy all had copies of the loan papers. Daddy's copy supposedly burned up in the Corvette when he was killed. The other copies somehow never surfaced, but Ova Blanton, Ray's mother, admitted to Mamaw that she knew that her son had maneuvered out of their obligation and that she felt bad about it. She apparently had no way to pay back the money herself, but she felt sorry about the wrong being done by her son. Without any paperwork, there was nothing to be done.

After Larry Britt had been entrenched with our family for a couple of years, I was so frustrated and desperate to get out from under all of that anguish and have my own family that I fell in love (or what I thought at the time was love) and got married in April 1977, just two months after the Britt trial and judgment.

Because I was barely sixteen, my grandmother had to grant written permission. We were married by the justice of the peace, went to Memphis for the night for our honeymoon, and came back and went to school on Monday. I still lived in the same house. My grandmother moved into the house's basement addition that Daddy had built and lived in during his last few years. I finally forced Britt to move out, because legally it was my house. Britt went to Nashville and had various jobs. In 1986, he was found murdered by a shotgun blast to the head at the company where he was working as a night watchman.

While all of this real-life drama was going on, the two *Walking Tall* sequels were filmed and hit the box office. Both films, like the original, were shot in Chester County and Madison County. Likewise, the same actors as in the original film were playing four members of our family. Noah Beery, Jr., played my grandfather, Lurene Tuttle played my grandmother, Leif Garrett played Mike, and Dawn Lyn played me in both 1975's *Part II—Walking Tall,* which originally was to have been called *Buford,* and in 1977's *The Final Chapter—Walking Tall.*

The big change was, of course, that my Daddy did not play himself as had been planned for the first sequel. Actor Bo Svenson played Daddy's part. I was not particularly impressed with his portrayal of my daddy. He was no Joe Don Baker, who I thought did such a good job in the role for the first movie.

I met Svenson at a pre-production party after Daddy died. I was so excited that I was going to get to meet him. Immediately, I started thinking about a father figure, because I remembered how Joe Don Baker had been so nice to me. I loved him so dearly.

I was thinking all these things. I had always been a big-sized girl. Svenson walked into the party, and I was just so thrilled to see him. The party host said, "Bo Svenson, I would like to introduce you to Buford Pusser's daughter. This is Dwana Pusser."

Svenson responded, "Well, hey, looks like you need to go on a diet, don't you?"

That absolutely broke my heart, because I was already looking up to him as my father figure—as any little girl would do toward the man who was going to play her daddy. The producers and director got a hold of Svenson and gave him a good going over.

I burst into tears and ran to the restroom. I stayed away from Svenson after that. We knew not to cross paths.

I had a better experience with Brian Dennehy, who played the part of my daddy in the *Walking Tall* TV movie in 1978. He was a nice man and very cordial.

Both of the feature films did O.K. at the box office, but critics and fans alike still greatly preferred the original. That holds true to this day. Most of my memories about watching the filming are just my being impressed by the general excitement of having a Hollywood film crew working in our area. I don't have many significant recollections about specific things that happened.

There was also a 1981 TV series on NBC that lasted for about six months. It also starred Bo Svenson, but none of the other cast from the movies. It was filmed entirely in Hollywood and was pretty forgettable.

Frankly, my real life was busy enough and left me with little time to focus on those movies. My daddy's estate did get residuals from the films. Every little bit helped, especially when the Larry Britt sinkhole was sucking away our funds.

I had wasted no time in getting my new family started. After my marriage in April 1977, my first daughter, Atoyia, was born in December. As any parent knows, having a child, especially your first, is an emotional, exciting, and scary experience—particularly when you're still a month shy of your seventeenth birthday.

Exactly a week before my seventeenth birthday, on January 2, 1978, Papaw died. He had been in declining health for many years. He suffered greatly with arthritis. He also had heart problems for years. He died of heart failure and the combination of living hard and old age. It was a difficult loss, of course, but compared to the premature deaths of both my mother and my daddy, it was more the natural course of life. I grieved over losing him, but it wasn't the agonizing grief I had over losing my parents.

With a newborn daughter to take care of, I also didn't have the luxury of prolonged grieving.

Lloyd Harris, my grandmother's brother, became my first homebound teacher as I took care of Atoyia. (The school system would provide a teacher to come to your home if you were seriously disabled or had small children to take care of and that sort of thing.) After that, John Lee Powers became my homebound teacher for my senior year. I couldn't have asked for two better people to come into my life and teach me not only what was in the books but also about living. They were a godsend because I was young and vulnerable and naïve about a lot of things and didn't have a daddy anymore.

I tried to go back to attending regular classes at Adamsville High my senior year, but because of all that I had been through with becoming a mother, I had matured a lot more during my junior year than my classmates. I lasted for only about a month. The teacher could tell I was just too restless to be in a classroom anymore. She asked me if I'd like her to sign the papers to allow me to finish out my senior year as a homebound student. I said, "Oh yes, please!" I wanted so much to be home with my daughter, which was something my fellow students couldn't really comprehend, nor should I have expected them to. I finished my senior year with homebound study and graduated with my class in 1979.

Around 1980, I took an Emergency Medical Certification course because I wanted to be more prepared for medical emergencies and to be able to help people. I'm sure that the various medical traumas of my daddy's life, and especially the ways that both he and my mother died, were key factors in my wanting to get that certification. My grandmother also had some medical problems, including a broken hip, so I wanted to be more prepared to help her if something were to happen. I also just had this desire within me to want to help people. I think it was in part because I could identify so well with people who were suffering. If someone was in pain, I usually knew exactly what they were feeling from personal experience, and I wanted to help stop it.

Sometimes I was the one who needed the medical attention. On a trip to Louisville to visit my mother's family in the early 1980s, I was driving and we had a car wreck—just running off the road or a rear-ending or something not very serious. I don't remember exactly what happened. But the accident was serious enough that my head hit the windshield and the car got torn up pretty bad.

After the accident, I was more focused on finding work and making money to help support my family. I worked for a while at Coleman's Barbecue in Selmer. I'd go there very early in the morning to make the biscuits in much the same way that my grandmother had taught me to make them at home.

I was too young when I got married the first time. I so badly wanted a family, but it had become an abusive marriage. I was finally maturing to where I understood that what was going on was not right.

At church one day, I met a lady named Gwen Gibson. She happened to be the niece of Red West, a close friend of Elvis Presley as well as one of his bodyguards. Her husband was from Adamsville and they were visiting for the weekend. She said, "I can tell by looking at you that you're hurting. I'm not a counselor, but maybe I can be of help to you. I've written down my phone number and my address. If I can be a friend to you, please let me know."

Before long, I took another beating. I thought, "This is it. I've got to get out of this situation." I headed out to Memphis and stopped to call Gwen on the way. She met me at a Chuck E. Cheese's in Memphis. I spent the weekend at her home. She said, "If you go back there and try one more time, you'll know you've done everything you can do."

So I gave it one more try. My husband and I got counseling. But about three weeks later, he started in again with the verbal and physical abuse. I had gotten in the habit of leaving my keys by the door, so they would always be in the same place and I could grab them if I ever needed to leave in a hurry. I went to Mamaw's room, where both she and Atoyia were. I grabbed Atoyia and told Mamaw to lock her door. I knew my husband wouldn't hurt her.

Atoyia and I got in the car and left for good.

CHAPTER 15

Losing and Finding My Way in Life

My first husband and I were divorced in 1983. A lot of people just assumed that I didn't need to make money, but they didn't know all that had gone on with Larry Britt. I did need to make money and I needed to work. In fact, after my divorce, I worked two and sometimes three jobs just to keep things going. I worked at the Garan shirt factory for about two months, then went back to Coleman's Barbecue, and then went on to work as a hostess for a new, really nice restaurant in Adamsville called Chadwick's.

This was also a period of my life when I was living so dangerously that I must have subconsciously wanted to get hurt. With my first taste of freedom, I immediately started going with my girlfriends to dances in Corinth. Before long, I started dating a man mainly because he was an ex-con and drove a red Corvette. Of course, in my life, it could never be just that simple. Men with the Criminal Investigation Division of the Highway Patrol immediately paid me a visit and asked me to keep dating this man. They wanted me to get some information about his operations. They suspected that he had an automobile "chop shop" and that he was perhaps involved in other criminal activities. That was just what my life needed—criminal intrigue!

One night I accidentally saw the chop-shop operation when I was visiting the man's business. A truck happened to come in and was immediately being dismantled before it could be blocked from my view. The man wasn't positive that I saw anything. Nevertheless, he took me out to a bridge in the boonies and told me that a lot of people had gone off that bridge and not by choice and that if I had seen anything, then the cops would come after both of us. I assured him that I hadn't seen anything, and he took me back home for the night.

After that, I seemed to always have to work a lot and just never could quite get free for more dates with this man. That was just as well, because it wasn't much longer before he was arrested and ended up serving time in jail. After he got out of jail, I would run into him around the area. We were just cordial. Nothing more was ever said between us about his activities or mine. I think we both knew to leave a closed book closed.

In 1984, I began a serious relationship with a man named Keith. It was probably my first time being in love, because before, when I thought I was in love and had gotten married, I was really too young to know.

Keith was doing construction work, and the company he worked for needed a minority to fill a quota on a certain job. Since women were considered a minority, I got the job and worked construction for a while. It was actually more like destruction. The job was busting out old walls and ceilings in a school. Of course, knowing my luck, it had to be asbestos that we were removing. We were given masks and gloves, but the precautions for working around asbestos at that time weren't what they are today.

Then I got my first real break with a job that could be considered the start of an actual career. A friend suggested to a radio station in Savannah, Tennessee, that they hire me as an ad salesperson. The station had an opening for one sales position. The sales manager set up a competition between me and another person. Whoever sold the most ads during a two-month trial would get not only the job, but a snazzy satin jacket with the station's logo. A satin jacket—wow!

I earned that jacket and ended up working at the radio station for fifteen years. Owner Mel Carnal was like a second father to me. When the on-air personality didn't show up one afternoon, the manager in charge said that I would have to go on the air to fill in. Up to that point, the most I had done on air was a few taped commercials. Being on air "live" was a completely different thing.

And that's not to mention that growing up, I, like my daddy, had always had a little bit of a speech impediment. I did the Barbara Walters sort of thing where "Roy Rogers Roast Beef" would come out "Woy Wogers Woast Beef." I was the last person anybody would ever have expected to be in broadcasting. I was scared to death, but they insisted and so I did it. I settled down and eventually got the hang of it. I went on to do the afternoon drive-time slot and ultimately had a morning show with Mel.

During the last three years of my radio career, I was also working as a liaison between the doctors and nurses and the patients for a home health company. It was supposed to be a marketing job, but it was really more like public relations and being a patient advocate. Between my radio ad sales and healthcare work, I was driving about fifty thousand miles a year. I also had earned my insurance license and was selling cell phones. Just like my daddy, I love to drive a car. I covered a lot of territory working my jobs. I drove so much one year that I actually got tarsal tunnel syndrome. Most folks get carpal tunnel syndrome from too many repetitive tasks with their hands. I got tarsal tunnel from too much pedal work with my right foot.

I was on the go so much with trying to make ends meet that Atoyia still slept with her great-grandmother, my mamaw. When Mamaw died on New Year's Day 1987, I was devastated. She died at the house. She had been admitted to the hospital, but she wanted to come home. The doctors had found that she had a blood clot, and it moved New Year's Eve. She died a few minutes after midnight.

I couldn't grieve properly for Mamaw's death because I needed to be strong and carry on for Atoyia. The sadness was overwhelming. Mamaw had been such a central part of my life, especially after my mother's death and even more so after Daddy's death. And now she was gone, too.

Another family member was having trouble accepting Mamaw's death, too. Our Great Dane, Shadow, simply didn't understand. While my grandmother was still alive, I had rented another house in town where I was staying. I could never get Shadow to stay at that house. I'd put her in the car and take her over to my new house, but she'd come back because my grandmother was still at our other house. For three or four weeks after my grandmother died, I had to keep going over to our old house and bring Shadow back. She kept wanting to go home and wait for Mamaw. One morning I woke up at the new house, and there Shadow was. It looked as though this dog had cried and cried. I think she had finally realized that Mamaw wasn't coming back.

That following March, I pretty much had a nervous breakdown. Three days before my planned marriage to Keith, we called off the wedding. Combined with my grandmother's death, this decision really threw me for a loop. It seemed that my life was falling apart around me.

During this time, I had moved to Savannah, where I was working for the radio station. I was so depressed after my grandmother had died and the relationship I was in had broken up that I was just ready for the pain to end. If a very good friend, Tony Barham, had not come knocking on my door one day, I doubt I would be here today.

I was taking Prozac, but I really believe it had a reverse effect on me and made me want to kill myself. Tony had stopped by the house to use the telephone. I was cleaning my .357 magnum in the bedroom and was getting ready to take my life. The only way my friend got into the house was that I had left the side door unlocked to make it easier for someone to find me.

Tony took me to my doctor, who got me into counseling. I've always tried to sort out my own problems. I'm thankful that this time, when I failed to do that and was about to end it all, the Lord sent Tony to find me before it was too late.

I'm also grateful that I then received the counseling that helped me find my way again.

In the summer of 1987, I married my second husband. He is the biological father of my beautiful daughter, Madison. Three days after giving birth to Madison in 1990, I couldn't walk. The doctors put me back in the hospital and thought at first that my inability to walk was just an aftereffect of the epidural. I found out differently later.

My second marriage was rocky. He was a police officer and wore that badge, just as Daddy had. But my grandmother always said everything that glitters is not always gold, and how I found that out.

He had an alcohol addiction. At the time we married, I didn't even know that he drank much. The drinking got worse and worse, and there was mental abuse. Then he proved to be unfaithful. I wasn't the one he wanted to come home to.

I gave him numerous chances. I'd let him come back, and I'd forgive him. I believe in marriage and I did everything from my side to keep ours alive, but one person doesn't make a marriage. So in 1992, we divorced.

He died in 2007. The one great blessing and gift of that marriage was the birth of Madison. For that alone, I'm forever thankful for that marriage. But it was time to move on and to move back to Adamsville.

I had lived in Savannah for a long time. I see now that I needed to live away from Adamsville to learn to be my own person. In Savannah, I wasn't Buford Pusser's daughter. Even though Savannah is only eight miles from Adamsville, I was able to become my own person. I'm sure that has been a good thing in my healing and my growing and in the way that I am now able to handle being the daughter of a very famous man. I can embrace it now in ways I never could have if I had not gotten away and found my own way, mistakes and all, for a few years.

Atoyia and I together had beaten the odds of my having her when I was so young and then largely raising her as a single mom. Atoyia graduated high school with honors. We moved back to Adamsville. She went on to get her nursing degree. She is married to a good man and is living a good Christian life. She and her husband have a wonderful little boy, my first grandson, Hayse, which was my daddy's middle name.

When I first moved back to Adamsville with Atoyia and Madison, a city commissioner had recently moved out of town. In high school, I always had an interest in civics. I guess my interest was another extension of my having watched and been a part of my daddy's campaigning through the years. Politics had always interested me. Anyway, Mayor Paul Wallace Plunk and the city commission needed to appoint a new commissioner to serve out the departing commissioner's term. They selected me.

I've since been elected for additional terms. I've also run for mayor, but was defeated—ironically by the same man whose city commissioner term I had completed. He had moved back to town. He was also the same man Daddy had

My girls and me (from left): Madison, me, and Atoyia.

beaten in the constable's race in 1962. It's a small world, especially in a small town.

Around this time I began dating a man named Jamie Garrison. He had lived nearby when I was growing up. As a young girl, I had a crush on him. As it turned out, I still did. We were married in 1998. He adopted Madison and has been a devoted father to her. I love Tara, his daughter by his first marriage, and her husband. They have two daughters, Abby and Danibeth, whom I love as if they were my own grandchildren.

That same year, I decided to leave the home health business and open my own restaurant, Pusser's Restaurant, in downtown Adamsville. It was located in the old Walker's Grocery Store on Main Street.

Mr. Walker went out of business and was auctioning off the items in the store. Jamie and I just happened to be out riding bicycles the night of the auction. That's how it is in Adamsville. I've always explained to people that it's kind of like Mayberry. You can just get out at night and walk up and down the sidewalks. You don't have to worry. Anyway, I went into the building to see what they were auctioning. We bought

Pusser's Restaurant at night, Main Street, Adamsville, Tennessee. (Photograph by Wiley Brewer)

all kinds of stuff, including cans of hominy and cleaning supplies that we still haven't used. As we were bidding and winning, Jamie looked at me and asked, "Do you have any money on you?" I said no. He got back on his bicycle and rode home. He drove back in our truck and brought some money.

During the auction, I kept looking at the building and thinking what a shame it was for Adamsville to lose this business in the heart of downtown. Within a couple of months, I came up with the restaurant idea. Within five weeks after that, we took an old building and transformed it into our restaurant. I was mulling over what to call the restaurant. I thought about calling it Pusser's, but worried about whether that would stir up too many painful memories for me, with people coming in on a daily basis and wanting to talk about my daddy and his legend.

I knew that good food and service would draw locals, but I also knew that the name Pusser would draw tourists. And a restaurant needs every advantage it can muster in order to succeed. And so Pusser's it was.

We opened the restaurant in July 1998. I felt good about what we were doing. People in Adamsville had a nice, new place to go eat. The city was getting new tax revenues, a vibrant business was added to downtown, and we were employing people. Most of all, I enjoyed restaurant work.

I talked this venture over with Mel at the radio station. He said he wanted me to stay on with the radio show. For a while, I did the radio show in the morning and ran the restaurant the rest of the day.

One day after I returned to the radio station after three days of vacation, I found out that Mel, who is about thirty years older than I am, was retiring at the end of the next week. And that wasn't all. While I was gone, the decision had been made that I would be retiring, too. I was completely shocked and devastated. I made it through the Thursday and Friday shows that week and had the weekend to think about what to do.

During my show on Monday, I told my listeners that I was being retired with Mel at the end of the week. I then said that, given the abruptness of the news to me, that day's show would be my last. I thanked my listeners for their loyalty and friendship during the last fifteen years. We cut to the news. I grabbed my purse and left. I bawled and cried all the way home. Then I had to go and open the restaurant. At the end of the day, I went home and bawled and cried some more.

Of all of the things that had happened in my life, being let go from that job—and not because of poor job performance— was one of the worst. It was something I had worked at very hard for fifteen years and had invested a lot of emotional energy in. Suddenly it was just cut off. It was like a death. Only it was lots of deaths, because I was separated from all of my listeners, many of whom I had gotten to know very well, just as they had gotten to know me. I may not have known their faces if they walked through the door, but I knew their voices.

I saw Mel for the first time years later. I said, "Mel, I don't know whether to hug you or slap you." I loved him but hated that he had so suddenly "retired" me when he had decided to retire.

He said, "Oh, please hug me. I'm getting too old to slap, even though I deserve it." I think he just hadn't known how to break the news about having to let me go from the radio station. It had been as hard on him as it had been on me. I hugged him.

With the loss of my radio career, I threw myself into my work at the restaurant. By the end of October, I got to where my back and legs hurt so much, I could barely walk. I went to my chiropractor and said, "You've just got to do something for me."

He put me on the examination table and he did a few things. Then he went out, came back, and said, "You're going to a neurologist tomorrow. I've already made an appointment for you."

I asked, "What am I going to a neurologist for? You've always fixed me."

He said he didn't like some of the symptoms that I was showing. One test he did was to stick needles in my feet. I didn't flinch and didn't even know he had done it.

I went to a neurologist in Jackson who examined me and talked with me for a long time. She said, "We won't know for sure until we run some more tests, but I think you have multiple sclerosis."

I wasn't quite ready to accept the diagnosis. It was only later that I began putting together any pieces to the MS puzzle or even knowing that there was an MS puzzle.

I thought back to that car accident in the early 1980s when I bumped my head against the windshield. I had gotten checked out at the hospital and everything seemed fine, so we had headed on toward Louisville the next day. We had just barely started out when my vision started blurring and my right arm went numb. We turned around and went to the hospital in Jackson. The doctors at the time thought the symptoms were just from the concussion. My doctors now think that the symptoms might have been the initial signs of multiple sclerosis, which often shows its first symptoms after an injury or some sort of trauma to the body. As I later learned more about this mysterious disease and began to think back, I also wondered if the MS might have been associated with my inner-ear symptoms during childhood and the emotional trauma of things that happened to our family.

My doctors would come to believe that, back in 1990, when I had had problems walking after Madison was born, it had been an exacerbation of the MS brought on by giving birth. Eight years later, I was still in denial about possibly having MS. It was mentioned to me, but I just didn't want to think about it.

With the new diagnosis, I tried bed rest for a few weeks, which, as it turns out, my particular MS responds to very well. I then went back to working like a dog at the restaurant. By February, the MS was ready to throw another punch, and I went down again.

This time, my chiropractor sent me to a specialist in

Birmingham. Maybe I would finally accept the diagnosis if it came from a doctor who was out of state. I again flunked all of the neurological needle tests and a bunch of others. The doctor told my family, "Whatever it is, she's going to be paralyzed if we don't do something for her."

The doctor brought in two other doctors, and they all concurred that it was multiple sclerosis. They agreed that a scan of my brain revealed a lesion that indicated that the MS had progressed to another stage. So that's where I am today. Even when I don't feel my best, people tell me that I don't look as if I'm sick. I reply, "'Paint and powder' does a lot."

I now understood that I needed to adjust my lifestyle and my work. I had been slow to follow doctors' orders—or anybody else's, for that matter. And I still go through lots of periods of going full speed, followed by total collapse as I succumb to symptoms. After a period of rest, I'm right back at it. I'm trying to learn to live life at a steadier pace. It's not my natural personality to live that way, but the MS is a pretty strict disciplinarian. Fortunately, I continue to have friends, a family, and a faith that give me strength and encouragement to overcome obstacles.

Throughout my life, many of the people closest to me and who are like family to me have not been "blood kin." Norma Woods is one. She helped raise me. Ronald Hardin is another. He was my next-door neighbor when I moved to Savannah and is still a dear friend. And then there's Shirley Sparks. We call her Mama Shirley. We couldn't have raised Madison without her help. She has been a constant friend and confidante. I love these people more than life itself. I see people who are "like family" to me as being a real family to me. The distinction of who is family is, for me, more about how you treat each other and the love and respect you have for each other. If you love and are loved by somebody, that's family. Our family never has been one to dissect bloodlines too much.

In the same way that people have helped me and been a friend to me, I feel a tug to reach out to people who maybe have been a little down on their luck and are just looking for a chance. A case in point is a very special and outstanding person who had just gotten out of drug rehabilitation when she came to work for us at the restaurant. Nobody would give her another chance. She had lost custody of her daughters. She was living in a run-down trailer. We gave her a chance at the restaurant, and I am so proud of her. She beat her addiction. She got her girls back. She went from the trailer and now has a nice home. She pays her bills on time, keeps her house spotless, and takes care of her kids.

I think sometimes I can't handle all the difficulties and hard work of life anymore. I just get tired and feel as though I can't take the stress. Then I think about people like this lady, who has worked to overcome such extraordinary personal adversity and has triumphed. Not only does it help me put my own life in perspective, but I can see that maybe sometimes I've done something that has made a positive difference in somebody else's life. And my daddy has indirectly made a difference for that person, too. Had it not been for my daddy and the way that he treated people, I don't think I would be the way I am today.

We sold Pusser's Restaurant in March 2006. Despite having lots of satisfied customers and being a positive force in so many of our lives, the restaurant was losing money. The restaurant business is difficult in the best of circumstances. And we probably didn't run the business with as much an eye to the bottom line as we could have. It was a difficult decision. In the end, I realized that selling it was the right thing to do. The new owners changed the name and concept. They also couldn't make a go of it, and closed the restaurant in the summer of 2007.

A lot of people and places have come and gone in my life. My faith has been one constant. Had I not been brought up in the church and had the morals and faith and support that it provided, I don't believe there is any way I could have made it to this point. There were times when I barely squeaked by, even with my faith.

Being involved in the drug scene would have been an easy thing for me to have done as a teenager, because drugs were all around us—just as they are for kids today. (Times had certainly changed from my daddy's day when whiskey was just about the most serious mind-altering substance you had to worry about in McNairy County.) But using drugs would have been a cop-out, and that wasn't how I was raised. I was brought up to believe that you are responsible for your actions.

Though I was raised in the Church of Christ, I'm now a member of the Baptist church. Madison joined the Baptist church first, and then I joined. Even though the Church of Christ we attended had been my church home all of my life, I had been thinking about looking for another church to join.

About that time, which was also around the time that the massacre happened at Columbine High School in Colorado, Madison attended a revival at the Baptist church and became saved and joined that church. At first, I was shocked and had the knee-jerk reaction that my daughter had been taken away from me. But then I came to realize the depth of her convictions and took a closer look at the Baptist church for myself. I joined the Baptist church and it has been a real blessing to me.

I know I'm still finding my way in life. I suppose most of us are constantly doing that. That's just life. I've survived family tragedies and heartaches. I've also made some wrong turns and hit some dead ends, but I believe that the sum of my experiences, pleasant and unpleasant, has given me the strength that I have today.

I'm proud of my heritage and blessed with a family that I love. We're involved with a church that nourishes our spirits. I'm pleased to have the chance to contribute to my community through civic involvement. I know there will be both good times and bad down the road, just as there are plenty of both in my rearview mirror. But if I buckle up, keep my eyes on the road, and try to obey the speed limits, I now believe I'll be able to enjoy the rest of the ride.

CHAPTER 16

Preserving My Daddy's Legacy: The Buford Pusser Home and Museum

Several things spurred me on during the early 1980s to try to turn Daddy's house—our home—into a museum. One was that I still saw our home as a target. I had a small child and worried that somebody might try to kidnap her. There actually had been a few threats.

Another reason came knocking at the door. My first husband answered the knock.

"I'm with the Internal Revenue Service. I need to talk to you," the man at the door said.

He came in and proceeded to tell me, "Your father's estate may be required to pay $38,000 in taxes. Apparently, no one has ever paid any taxes on the money the estate paid out to you each month to live on. They never told you. Lady, you'd better come up with the money."

I told him, "You can't squeeze blood from a turnip."

He said, "You wanna watch me?"

I knew I didn't want to be squeezed that hard. I needed to find somebody who would let me take out a loan on our house to pay the taxes. Central Bank in Savannah, Tennessee, came to my rescue. The first payment was $382. My grandmother drew only maybe $300 a month from her pension. I got divorced and went to work at Coleman's Barbecue down the street to help us pay bills. When I eventually did get paid by the estate, I wound up receiving a sum of just under $4,000.

What happened to what should have been a $500,000

estate? I could only guess. The clerks at the courthouse went through the estate and paid out various expenses. For example, they paid Lloyd Tatum, my daddy's attorney, $10,000 just because he wasn't going to be my daddy's attorney anymore. They thought he deserved that. Tatum also still gets a quarter of every dollar of royalties earned in rights from the various *Walking Tall* projects, so he's doing O.K.

The bottom line was that I needed the money, and the house was the single largest and, for all practical purposes, the only tangible asset I had.

Another reason for my wanting to move out of the house and make it into a museum was that a constant stream of visitors seemed to be searching for something that could serve as a shrine to my father. I know that was so, because they came knocking on our door like the tax man. Every day, all hours of the day, morning, noon, and night, they'd knock on the door and ask if this was where Buford Pusser lived. "Someone where I live told me they came through here and saw his house," they'd say.

They would stop by and Mamaw would invite them to come in. Word spread that my grandmother would do this, so people from all over the United States would come traipsing through. Most were very nice folks and keen on Daddy. That part was O.K. They were sincere and respectful. Some folks apparently weren't as nice, because all sorts of our possessions turned up missing and became souvenirs for less respectful visitors. That wasn't O.K.

Once I was married and had a child, it was just very hard to live a normal life at that house. Early one morning when I was cooking breakfast, some people came knocking on the door wanting to come in. There I was in my gown. I thought, "This is not a hotel. This is not a place where people should just come around whenever they want. It isn't a public place. How am I going to do this?" It was getting worse, and evidently my grandmother was just going to let them keep coming inside. We had to find a better way of managing people's interest in visiting our home.

My biggest motivation for starting the museum was simply my desire to honor my father. What really got me thinking along those lines for the first time was some advice from Gwen Gibson, the same wise lady who had wakened in me the understanding about how to deal with the problems in my first marriage.

Gwen said to me, "Let me tell you something about your daddy. Listen to me closely. You can take his legend and bury it where it is now—right there in the cemetery in Adamsville. But your daddy left you something that most people can only read about in a book. He left you a legend. It's up to you to do with that legend whatever you decide. You can take it and run with it and make the best of it. Make that home into a museum. Do anything you can to preserve the legend. You can either let it die in the ground or you can take it and run with it. The choice is yours because it's your birthright."

That's where I got the inspiration for my decision to turn the house into a museum. It would take three years, the shedding of many tears, and lots of sweat and hard work by several dedicated people, but we finally made the deal to transform the house into a museum.

After returning home from my visit with Gwen, I was fired up to make the dream of the museum a reality. I wondered how to go about it. I was young and naïve. I visited our state representative, Herman Wolf. He just laughed at the idea of it. The state had put a marker up at the spot where Daddy was killed. He couldn't imagine the state doing anything more than that, but nevertheless he agreed to introduce the proposal in the legislature.

House Speaker (and future governor) Ned Ray McWherter, Lt. Gov. John Wilder, and State Trooper Steve Browder (a native of McNairy County and also McWherter's bodyguard) are the ones who really pushed for the museum. It took a lot of begging, pleading, praying, running into brick walls and falling down, and then getting up and going around another way. After three years, the legislature went for the idea and agreed to purchase the house. They bought our house and the Lorraine Motel in Memphis, where Dr. Martin Luther King, Jr., was assassinated.

Steve Browder was my connection. He was the one helping me in Nashville by taking the proposal from office to office and various committees. It was a real civics lesson for me. Steve stayed on top of the bill and personally delivered the proposed legislation from one place to the other. Even with all of our efforts, it still took three years.

The first time the bill was brought before the legislature, Speaker McWherter had been in his office. Without him there, it didn't pass. Steve ran down to the speaker's office and said, "Mr. Speaker, they just put the bill up and they killed it."

Without a word, McWherter went up the hall to the chamber. He walked straight up the aisle, took the podium, and said (I'm paraphrasing), "We're gonna back up here. I can look out here over this crowd right now, and I can start pointing fingers and naming names of those who wanted to be Buford Pusser's best friend when he was alive. I remember different rallies where we were together and seeing who was acting like Buford Pusser was their best buddy. Now we have the opportunity to keep a piece of history and to let his story continue, and you're just going to let it go? I think you need to rethink it. We're revoting."

The bill passed.

That's why I owe so much of what we have with the museum and the preservation of Daddy's legacy to Ned Ray McWherter. He's a stand-up person. If somebody called tomorrow and said that Mr. McWherter needed one of my kidneys or an eye, if I could do anything for that man, I would. When my daddy was no longer around to speak for himself, Ned Ray McWherter and Steve Browder stood up for him and pushed and pushed to see that the museum got done.

The state purchased our house in 1987 and gave it to the City of Adamsville, which is allowed to keep the house as long as it remains a museum. If that status ever changes,

The Sheriff Buford Pusser Home and Museum in Adamsville, Tennessee. (Photograph by Wiley Brewer)

then the city is required either to give it back to the state or pay the state back the $170,000 it paid for the house.

Though my grandmother, who died in January 1987, would never get to see the house become a museum, she knew that everything was in place for the eventual switch from home to museum. She was both proud and excited to know that the house and the memory of her son were going to be preserved. It was satisfying for me, too. After all the trouble I caused and all the misery I had put my grandmother through, I do know that I did this one thing that totally pleased her.

I feel an obligation to make sure that the museum keeps going. Of course, there are some days I don't want to be a part of this whole story. I don't want to be Buford Pusser's daughter. I don't want to be any part of this hoopla and turmoil that has taken place in my life. I'd like to just shut my eyes and believe, "Everything that happened was just a movie that I went to last week." I don't usually have those thoughts unless I'm very depressed and sad for some reason, or when I'm upset or just plain exhausted. But I just take a big breath and I think about it. I can't just walk away from it. It's my father's legacy and mine, and my family's. There are also a lot of people who have it a lot worse than I've had it. I think about that and usually get off my pity party pretty darned fast.

When I visit what was our home and is now the museum for any length of time, I usually end up getting very emotional because so many powerful memories just keep rushing back. Some people wonder why I don't hang out at the house in my spare time or at least visit more often. The reason is that it's such a personal and sometimes traumatic experience.

Walking around the house, I'll see things like the kitchen and immediately picture Daddy or Mamaw cooking at what was a state-of-the-art Jenn-Air range. Daddy in particular loved that. I can also still visualize all of us sitting around the kitchen table and having a meal together.

On down the hall, my room is the first room on the right. The room has a painted white dresser that was one of the first pieces of furniture that my parents owned. The bed is the one that had been in their bedroom, where I was sleeping the morning my mother was murdered.

At the end of the hall is Mike's bedroom. Lots of his personal items are there from his teenage years. Even though my grandmother continued to live in the house for many years after Daddy's death, it's like a time warp to see how much is just frozen in time at the moment when Daddy died.

I sometimes hear people talk about Graceland and how atrocious some of the décor and items are that Elvis had. Elvis is stuck in time, too. I suppose that, from a decorating and fashion standpoint, the 1970s are an unfortunate time to be stuck in forever. I'm sure the yellow shag carpeting in our house can go toe to toe with Elvis's. But being stuck in time is part of the point of preserving a home and having a museum, whether it be our humble home or Graceland.

For most visitors to the museum, the downstairs is what really grabs their attention, because that's where Daddy lived. In what was the living-room area of Daddy's bedroom suite, there are now display cases full of memorabilia and

That long-legged Daddy of mine stretches out while chatting on the telephone at home.

This is one of my favorite pictures of Daddy. Considering all of the surgeries he went through, I think that he was still a very handsome man.

personal items from his life. Some things, like mangled parts of the wrecked Corvette and the size-thirteen sneakers that he was wearing when he died, really hit me hard when I see them. They're morbid, but I guess they help people make a personal connection. Visitors also can browse through racks of news clippings about various events in Daddy's life and see some of his guns and other crime-fighting items.

But it's the small things that sometimes really get to me. I see the bottle of his Aramis cologne, and I'm immediately taken back to the aroma I smelled as a child when he hugged me. On a cabinet near his bed, eight-track tapes are stacked one atop the other. He had a definite bent toward country music. The tapes are by artists such as Ray Price, David Houston, Tammy Wynette, Freddy Hart, Sonny James, and Johnny Horton. I remember he would play Horton's tape over and over again. Of course, with an eight-track tape, that was especially easy to do. "North to Alaska"—if I heard Daddy play it once, I heard it 459 times. What I wouldn't give to hear him listen to it just once more.

Another song I remember him listening to a lot and really loving was Charlie Rich's "The Most Beautiful Girl." He loved anything by Charlie Rich, who was from Memphis, but that was his favorite one. Maybe it made him think of my mother. I like to think that it did.

And it goes without saying that Daddy loved Elvis's music, but I'll confirm it for the record. There's an eight-track tape of Elvis still on his dresser to prove it.

The bedroom also has a cedar-lined closet that's still full of Daddy's clothes. A visitor can glimpse in there and see just how big he was from his wardrobe. Many of his shirts were custom made. Many of his jackets have labels that say, *Especially made for Buford Pusser.*

A story about some of his shirts also involves the house itself. The man who lived across the street used to get into squabbles with his wife when maybe he had a drink or two too many. One time Daddy was asleep in our house when he heard someone yelling, "Buford! Buford, help me!" And then the voice would fade, come again, and fade once more. Soon, Daddy heard, "She's going to kill me, Buford!"

At first, Daddy couldn't decide whether he was dreaming or if the voice he heard was real. It was real. The poor man's wife was chasing him around the outside of our house with a broom. They would run down the side and then way around the backyard. That's why Daddy would hear it and then he wouldn't. He finally went outside and separated them.

He said to the woman, "Now, you know your husband has always done this, and I don't see it ending any time soon. Please don't kill him." The man, who was a patternmaker at the Garan factory, appreciated Daddy so much that when our house burned, he made Daddy a bunch of shirts and gave them to him.

Not all of Daddy's shirts fit him that well. There's a hot-pink tuxedo shirt still in his closet at the museum. Stuck in the seventies—and how! The shirt is from a time when Daddy was supposed to appear at an event associated with a rodeo. The organizers had rented him a tuxedo and picked out what they thought was a big-enough shirt. He got to the event and put on the tuxedo shirt. The shirttail didn't come even close to tucking in. It was the longest shirt they could find and not even close. Daddy said, "All I can tell you folks is that I can't wear it." This was a couple of hours before the event. Some enterprising person with a sewing machine found some fabric somewhere (probably from another shirt) and sewed about a six-inch tail on the shirt, saving the day and Daddy's dignity. That is, as much dignity as you can save for somebody who's wearing a hot-pink tuxedo shirt.

Around the corner from the closet is Daddy's deluxe bathroom. It may not look all that snazzy today, but in the 1970s it had the newest everything and was plumb irresistible—especially to a mischievous teenager.

When Daddy was out on the road, I'd love to sneak into his tub and take a bath. It's an extra-big, round tub and shower made by Aqua Glass, which is based in Adamsville. Today, Aqua Glass is known all over the world. The tub and the curved wall of the whole area were made with black Aqua Glass with white swirls. Daddy and Aqua Glass cofounder Lewis Cima made the tub together one Sunday.

I used to love to get in there, cover myself with soap suds, and then slide all the way around the walls. The only catch was that this would leave a soapy film all over the walls. Daddy had lectured me a couple of times about doing that.

One particular Saturday, Daddy wasn't expected to be home, so I had been down in his bathroom taking a shower and getting ready to go to a basketball game. It just so happened that, after I went upstairs, Daddy came home and decided to take a shower right away. I mentioned early in this book that my daddy whipped me only twice in my life—the first time being when I was tiny and was being taught a lesson for perching dangerously on a banister.

This was the second time.

When Daddy turned on the shower, the water and soap started running down the walls, because the soap hadn't dried from when I had taken a shower a little while earlier. He hollered, "Dwana!"

I sheepishly came down the stairs and stood, trembling, in my flimsy little housecoat. Daddy was there to greet me at the bottom of the stairs, rolling up a towel. "Dwana, what did I tell you about playing in that bathroom?" He kept rolling the towel. He popped my butt but good with that towel once, twice. I screamed and had the peepee scared out of me. He hollered, "Stop that!"

My grandmother came running out of the utility room next door and separated us as though we were a couple of kids.

Daddy said, "You're grounded!"

I asked for how long, and he responded, "For the rest of your life!"

I guess Daddy knew that the towel wouldn't really hurt me but just sting me enough to get his point across. I was surprised more than anything, because he hadn't whipped me since I was a toddler. My grandmother had given me switchings on what seemed like every other day with switches from the peach tree behind the house. And she'd make me go out to the tree to pick my own switches. I was used to my grandmother's switchings, and I deserved every one of them I got. Don't get me wrong—I was not an abused child. She should have whipped me twice a day, every day.

Anyway, Daddy eventually left the house, and Mamaw asked me what time I needed to be at the ballgame.

"But Daddy said I was grounded," I said.

She told me, "Oh, don't worry about it. Go on." My daddy may have been the law in McNairy County, but my grandmother was the law in our home.

I share that story for folks who might visit the museum and see that lavish bathtub. Now they'll know that there's a story that goes with it, and a painful one at that.

There's almost as much history outside in the yard of our home as there is inside. A lot of that history is literally buried there, because that's where we had our pet cemetery. Daddy's bulldogs, Old Bull and then Little Bull, are out there.

As I got older, Shadow, my Great Dane, would go over to the park down the block and watch ballgames. She would climb up on the bleachers and just sit there like a spectator. One day, this old man was sitting in the stands. He had a hotdog and a box of popcorn. He set his hotdog down and turned around to do something. When he looked back, his hotdog was gone and there sat Shadow with a satisfied look on her face. It scared the man. He probably thought he was next on the menu. Folks who knew Shadow quickly told the man, "No, that's just Shadow. She comes to the ballgames all the time. Just don't put food down around her. She'll gobble it up in a second. She loves people and she loves food."

Shadow lived to be about fourteen years old. She was living with me in Savannah when she finally died. I took her to the vet for something and found out that she was eaten up with cancer. I was bawling because I knew I'd have to put her to sleep. I called the City of Adamsville and asked if I could come back and bury her at our old home. They said I could. They even sent somebody to help dig the hole and bury her.

I also had a pony when I was a kid, and then, after I was an adult, I got a horse. The horse had a colt. It was an Appaloosa, one of the most gorgeous colts I've ever seen. There was a steep ditch out back that's now filled in and a lot shallower. It was icy one day and that poor colt slid down in there and couldn't get out. It must have broken its neck. We found it in there.

We also tried to keep a pet deer for a while. One day, some people called Daddy and said they had a baby deer. The mother deer had been shot, and the baby deer was eating their garden. Daddy went over there and got the deer, put it in the back of the police car, and brought it home to us. We kept the deer in our neighbor's small shed out back. We named the deer Bambi. As Bambi got bigger, Daddy worked very hard to build a large pen for her. He drove the posts and strung up a six-foot-tall fence around the backyard. He was so proud of his job well done. Daddy let Bambi out of the shed and she proceeded to jump right over the fence. Daddy was furious. Bambi was no fool, though. She came back.

Now it so happened that our neighbor's wife didn't allow him to drink in the house, so when he decided to have a drink, he'd go out to his shed and sit on the little porch that it had. He went out there one day, and Bambi jumped up on him to play. He had on overalls. Deer hooves are like razors. Bambi was just playing, but her hooves slid down through the overalls. When our neighbor came out of there, his bib overalls were shredded down to his knees. He was hollering and screaming. Bambi was just playing, but she had never done anything this dangerous before, so we had to get rid of her.

Daddy knew a man named Claude Jones in Savannah who kept some exotic animals on his big cattle farm. Claude and his farmhands built Bambi a nice big, tall cage and took her in. They also found out that Bambi was actually a boy. They changed his name to Buford. (They apparently didn't know that, male or female, any baby deer, including Disney's, can be a Bambi.) Claude and his crew would give the newly named Buford beer to drink and cigarette butts. He loved them. When he died years later, Buford's antlers had grown as big as a small tree.

The real trees in our backyard have also continued to grow over the years. That old peach tree, which I unfortunately helped prune and whose branches in turn helped discipline me, is still there. The sweet gum tree that my mother and daddy and I planted is also hanging in there. There are times when I just drive over to the house and sit and look at that tree. I look at its branches and see how they've grown just as I've grown—not just physically but mentally and spiritually. I look at the branches and see the different twists and turns that I've taken, and yet all of the branches lead back to the trunk. I can see my life in that tree. That may seem silly, but to be able to see something that my mother and father and I did together is somehow reassuring to me. Planting that tree is among the strongest memories that I have of the three of us doing something together. I've asked the City of Adamsville to please not ever cut it down.

CHAPTER 17

Walking Tall, 2004

It was the spring of 2003 when I first heard that MGM Studios was planning to do a remake of *Walking Tall.* It was a jolt. Then I heard that they were changing Daddy's name and not having the story set in Tennessee.

"So they can just change his name?" I asked. "I thought *Walking Tall* had to include the name Buford Pusser and his likeness."

I was told that was not the case. The studio had the right to change anything and everything about the story. They didn't have to set it in Tennessee. They could set it wherever they wanted to. Being Buford Pusser's daughter, plus having a little bit of a temper, I got very upset when I heard this. I started making contact with MGM, because I was trying to figure out all I could about what was going on. I'm sure the people at the movie studio thought, "What's this silly little country woman down there trying to do?"

I finally talked loudly enough and stomped around enough that I got somebody there to listen. The movie people started talking to me about the project, but by this time they were already filming it. Nevertheless, they arranged for me, my daughters, and Rex Robinson, my business manager, to fly to Vancouver, British Columbia, to watch some of the filming.

When some of the young guns at MGM first started working on the movie, I don't think it occurred to them that there was a family that was still protective of the real story or had feelings about how it was told. But that hitch in their think-ing would change as they got to know my family and me.

My daughters, Rex, and I spent two days on the set in Canada. We met The Rock, a.k.a. Dwayne Johnson, the wrestler-turned-movie star. He was very likeable and gra-cious to us. I could tell that he had a genuine interest in and respect for my father and his story. He asked me what I thought about his playing my father in the movie. I told him that I hadn't been sure about what kind of actor he was because I was mainly familiar with his wrestling career. But then I had rented a video of his film *The Scorpion King* and saw that he really did have talent as an actor, and I was more comfortable with him playing the role based on Daddy. After meeting Dwayne in person, I could tell he was very professional and focused about his work.

The first day we were on the set, they were filming the scene based on when my father first came back to the state line bar with his big stick to seek revenge for having been cheated out of his money, beaten, and left for dead. In the 2004 version, the scene is set in the Wild Cherry casino.

As we were watching the scene being filmed, we noticed that the crew was having to restart the action because some-thing was wrong. Then folks looked over our way and start-ed talking. I thought, "Oh, no, we've done something wrong. They're gonna kick us off the set the first ten minutes we're here." I just knew I was going to be in the same kind of trou-ble for disrupting production that I had gotten in on the set of the original *Walking Tall* three decades earlier.

But then Tanoai Reed, Dwayne's cousin and stunt double, came over and said, "Dwayne is so excited that you're here. This is a big scene, the first time he's come to stand up for what's right, and he really wants to do a good job—especial-ly since you're here." I guess our being there was making him nervous and he was missing his mark, which was prob-ably pretty easy to miss because he was required to do some very precise movements and action sequences. Of course, he soon got it right on target. But just the fact that it meant something to him for my family and me to be there told me that his heart was in the right place. In fact, he had hand-picked *Walking Tall* as the movie he wanted to do because the original movie had been one of his favorites when he was growing up.

Even though The Rock's heart was in the right place, at first I wasn't sure that the studio people completely understood the fallout that could result from what they were doing. The folks at MGM initially didn't see any big deal with the fact that they were changing the name of the main character from Buford Pusser to Chris Vaughn and changing the setting from Tennessee to Washington State. They saw the movie as just that, a movie that was inspired by my father's life and that incorporated a few of the basic events of his life.

In my mind, this was like telling the story of Daniel Boone but changing his name and having him wearing an armadillo cap while pioneering in Arizona. Oh, and while we're at it, let's make him an Apache.

You just don't tamper with a real-life legend. And that's not to mention that many people who remember the original *Walking Tall* (set in the South in the 1960s) and who also know about the real Buford Pusser might not buy into the notion that the main character of the new *Walking Tall* had a white mother and a black father.

The racial aspect wasn't so much an issue in and of itself (though it did show a lack of understanding of U.S. history) as it was one more confusing difference between the new *Walking Tall* and the life of the real Buford Pusser. Of course, I realized that the original *Walking Tall* and its sequels had plenty of Hollywood myth in them. But I didn't see a need for the new movie to change my daddy's name, his location, and even his skin color. All of the changes together were a big shock for me to absorb.

It wasn't until much later that I heard Dwayne Johnson himself explain in interviews that there were two main reasons why his character in the new movie wasn't called Buford Pusser. One was The Rock's own ethnicity. He's

African-American and Samoan. He simply doesn't look like somebody who would be named Buford Pusser. And the other reason was a respect for my daddy, the real story, and his legacy. The new movie was going to have more things different than the same about my daddy's life. For them to have kept the Buford Pusser name but changed so much else would have been disrespectful of the real story and the real man behind it.

Meanwhile, the people at MGM didn't seem to fully understand what they were getting into with *Walking Tall*. It was a decent-sized movie budget (more than fifty million dollars). They knew that. But they didn't seem to appreciate the depth to which the original movie and my father's legacy had touched people's lives. They were clued in a little bit when the limousine that they provided for us pulled up to our hotel in Vancouver. Eight or ten police cars were lined up with their lights flashing, and uniformed officers were standing there in the hotel driveway. The MGM people were asking, "What's going on?"

Rex said, "I think they're here for Dwana."

One of the MGM people asked, "Oh my god, what's she done now?"

Rex said, "No, you don't understand. They're here to show respect for her and her father because they know her through the National Sheriffs Association."

The MGM folks began to see a little more of the big picture. For my part, I also settled down and began to think everything through. We began to have a meeting of the minds. I slowly began to accept the new *Walking Tall*, and MGM began to understand me.

But in the end, it was the honesty, sincerity, and kindness of Dwayne Johnson that made me believe that the new film could do a good job of telling a story that was inspired by, if not exactly based on, my father's life, and that it could do so with dignity. The basic theme of good triumphing over evil was preserved. It was also a fact that MGM owned the movie rights to the title *Walking Tall*. They could legally do pretty much whatever they wanted with the title without my approval. Still, if they were to have smooth sailing at the box office, they knew they didn't need me rocking the boat. One Rock was enough for this film.

I also saw that if the movie became a success, it might spur the public's interest in learning more about the real story that inspired this new movie. Dwayne and the folks at MGM saw the same opportunity. With Dwayne's encouragement, they made plans for me to do interviews and appearances in support of the movie. The Rock would tell about the movie and what *Walking Tall* meant to him, and I would be able to say the new movie was good entertainment, which it is, while also going on to talk a little bit about the real life of the person who inspired this exciting movie.

I traveled to Los Angeles in early 2004 to see an advance cut of the movie. As I watched *Walking Tall* for the first time, I had too many thoughts in my mind to really watch the movie for what it is, which is entertainment. I was constantly comparing what I was seeing on the screen to real life—my life—so much so that all of the action taking place was simply lost on me. I got very upset.

Fortunately, I knew myself well enough to have requested the screening room for two separate viewings. Before the second viewing, I talked to Rex. He settled me down. He said, "Dwana, you've got a big decision to make about this movie. How you decide to handle this movie could affect the rest of your life."

I realized that Rex was right. I needed to try to distance myself emotionally from the new movie in order to see the situation more objectively—in a sense, to see the big picture. I was able to settle in and accept and enjoy the movie for what it is, which is a solid movie with good action, a very dignified performance by Dwayne Johnson, and good acting by the entire cast. The basic story was familiar, but it wasn't supposed to be a depiction of my daddy's life. I came to embrace the movie as something that could be a positive thing for my daddy's legacy.

And sure enough, something incredibly positive did happen that certainly never would have happened had there not been the new movie. And I doubt it would have happened if Dwayne Johnson hadn't been the star. Dwayne told the studio people and me that he not only wanted to come to McNairy County to promote the movie, but he insisted on it. I'm sure that his making such a trip was never in MGM's original plan for the movie's publicity tour. I think Dwayne's taking that stand really says a lot about his fine character.

It was arranged for Dwayne to come to Nashville on March 15, 2004, for the world premiere of his *Walking Tall* at the Regal Cinemas at Opry Mills. Two theaters side by side were filled with lots of family, friends, and public officials, many of whom had made the two-hour trip from McNairy County. Folks such as actor David Keith and country singers Mark Wills and Mark Collie also attended. Several members of the Tennessee Titans were there, too. Hundreds of excited fans turned out for the red-carpet entry.

I made a few remarks in both theaters before the film started. I was so overjoyed by seeing all of the family and friends that I could barely speak. Having all of these folks— some of whom knew my daddy—gathered together in one place for an event related to my daddy's life was an extremely emotional moment for me. I managed to rein in my emotions enough to give a proper introduction of The Rock, who was greeted with great enthusiasm. The audience loved the film, which made me feel good. I could tell the movie was going to have a positive impact.

After the screening, MGM hosted a nice party at the Gibson Bluegrass Showcase at Opry Mills. It was an all-American theme with hamburgers, hotdogs, and apple pie. My daddy would have eaten it up.

The next day, I flew with Dwayne and his entourage on their chartered Gulfstream from Nashville to McNairy County. I don't believe even my daddy ever traveled from Nashville to Selmer that fast. I didn't even have time to finish a can of Diet Coke between takeoff and landing.

Because of my multiple sclerosis, I worried about going down the stairs of the airplane. I said, "If I fall, I'll take out everybody in front of me."

From behind me I heard somebody say, "Don't worry, sis, I got your back." It was The Rock. Everybody laughed, and I got down the stairs without a problem.

We were greeted by a good-sized crowd of press and fans at the airport, but we quickly loaded into vehicles for the short trip to the courthouse in Selmer, where an official public ceremony was to be held.

The Rock rode in the middle of the backseat of a Suburban, with me seated on his left side and McNairy County mayor Mike Smith on his right. None of the three of us is little bitty, so it was pretty tight quarters.

To compound the discomfort, my MS was acting up some at that time. It was no wonder that the MS was flaring up with the strenuous schedule I had been keeping for several weeks in publicizing the movie. And the last few days in particular had been hectic. As we were riding to the courthouse, I began rubbing the tops of my thighs. I could feel the knots in them where the muscles had become all tightened. So I was rubbing and patting my legs continuously trying to get the soreness out, all the while wondering and worrying about whether anybody would show up for the ceremony at the courthouse. Plus I was thinking about my remarks for the ceremony, security, and so forth.

I suddenly realized that I couldn't feel any sensation in my right leg as I was rubbing it. I thought, "My poor old right leg has gone completely numb. I can't even feel it."

As I rubbed the leg with my right hand, I realized that, while the leg felt about the right size, it seemed to be a lot harder than my left thigh. I then looked down and realized that I hadn't been rubbing my right thigh. I had been rubbing The Rock's left leg. I looked up at him in total embarrassment. He just grinned and said, "I'd have let you know if you'd gone too far. I realized that you didn't have any idea. I saw that you were rubbing your leg and my leg and didn't know it."

"No, no! I had no idea," I apologized. "I just thought my leg had gone completely dead-numb. Our legs are about the same size, except that yours is a lot harder. I looked down and oh my gosh . . . "

I then just looked out the window and thought, "Well, we haven't been in McNairy County more than ten minutes and I've already molested the poor man." I was so embarrassed, but Dwayne knew it wasn't intentional.

We made our way to the McNairy County Courthouse in Selmer in the caravan of Sheriff's Department escorts. When we arrived at the courthouse, The Rock was greeted by hundreds of cheering fans. He spent probably ten or fifteen minutes walking the thirty yards from the car to the podium on the front steps of the courthouse. He signed every autograph he could reach, which was easily over a hundred.

When we finally reached the podium, I introduced Dwayne. He was made an honorary member of the McNairy County Sheriff's Department and was presented the key to the city. The highlight for me was when Dwayne made a presentation of his own. He presented a check for $5,000 on behalf of MGM and himself to the Buford Pusser Foundation. That was an extraordinarily generous gesture and a real boost for the foundation.

We then went inside and briefly toured the courthouse and my daddy's old office. Next we drove to Adamsville, where I gave Dwayne a quick tour of our house, now the Buford Pusser Home and Museum. Dwayne seemed genuinely interested in seeing the various pieces of memorabilia and learning more about my father. (One of the big sticks Dwayne used in his *Walking Tall* movie is now in the museum, too.)

Our last stop on this trip was a private gathering with my family and staff at our Pusser's Restaurant. The Rock had requested a special "training meal" for the lunch we served. It was two grilled chicken breasts, steamed vegetables, two baked potatoes, and a large salad. For everybody else, we had fried catfish and chicken fingers served family style with French fries, coleslaw, and hush puppies. We had a nice visit, and we had a chance to provide some real Southern food and hospitality for Dwayne and his entourage.

After lunch at Pusser's, The Rock and the MGM people

The Rock and I step away from the plane on the day he made the trip to McNairy County in March 2004. I took him to the courthouse where my Daddy's sheriff's office was, then to Adamsville to see our old home place and museum, and finally to lunch with my friends and staff at Pusser's Restaurant.

flew to Knoxville for another premiere of the movie. For my part, I spent the rest of the week virtually bedridden with my MS, which had become completely aggravated by all of the activity, excitement, and stress of the last few days. I was completely stove up. My doctor gave me some steroid shots that helped me get back on my feet. He said that, considering that I had been wrestling with The Rock all day, I was holding up pretty well.

The week after that, my family and I flew to Los Angeles for the West Coast premiere of *Walking Tall* at Grumman's Chinese Theater. It was spectacular—Hollywood glitz and glamor to the hilt. All of the movie's cast and crew were there, along with a lot of other movie stars and the usual army of paparazzi.

The biggest excitement for me at the Los Angeles premiere was actually at the hotel right before we left for the theater. For some reason, I was really emotional and anxious, but I didn't know why. I was standing on the balcony and hyperventilating. Something about being in Los Angeles for the premiere of *Walking Tall* was making me unsettled, but I couldn't quite put my finger on why that was the case.

About that time, the phone in the room rang and I answered.

The voice on the other end asked, "Dwana?"

I said, "Yes."

"Dwana, this is Joe Don Baker."

Though I was thrilled beyond belief to hear those words, I also immediately felt a tremendous calmness come over me. I asked Joe Don whether he was coming to the premiere, and he said that he had chosen not to attend, which I was of course sorry to hear. But I was still so happy just to hear his voice.

Trying not to get too choked up, I told him, "Oh, you don't know what it means for me to hear from you at this time. I had just been pacing here in the hotel room and feeling uneasy about even going to this premiere for some reason. But hearing from you is what I think is going to make it be all right."

I went on tell him, "I'm sorry to be so emotional. I was emotional even before you called. I just want you to know that, to me, you're the closest thing to my daddy. You knew my daddy, you were around us when you were making the movie, you were at Daddy's funeral, and you stayed in touch afterward. Every time I looked at you on TV, you were my daddy. You were the closest thing I had to a daddy after I was thirteen years old. Even though it has been several years since we've talked, I still feel that way. That I would hear from you right now, just when I'm having such mixed emotions about attending this premiere, must be a good sign."

With that call from Joe Don Baker, I felt that I had his blessings—that it was O.K. for me to enjoy the experience of the new *Walking Tall* and that it was not somehow a betrayal of him and of my daddy for me to be associated with the promotion of the new movie.

I went on to the premiere and to the party afterward. I enjoyed the festiveness and excitement of both. It was exciting to walk the red carpet in Hollywood—particularly for a premiere at Grumman's. The party was especially interesting because they decorated it with a lot of the vehicles and casino props from the movie.

The new *Walking Tall* movie went on to do O.K. at the box office (taking in over forty million dollars in the first month) and was another strong step forward in The Rock's transition from the wrestling ring to the movie screen.

Maybe my being out there as Buford Pusser's daughter in support of the movie made it a little easier for people familiar with the real story to swallow the scenarios of the new film. Of course, there was still controversy. But with controversy comes interest.

The excitement generated by the new movie—and especially the dynamic performance of The Rock—also indirectly helped bring the story of the real Buford Pusser in front of a lot more people who otherwise might never have known there even was a real story. For that, I'm grateful. We're all better for that. And I'm especially happy that the movie provided a vehicle for me and my family to meet and get to know The Rock, Dwayne Johnson, who is a truly fine person. I now consider him a good friend. If elements of my daddy's story were going to be changed for a movie, I'm glad that at the center of the action there was still a Rock.

Even so, I still can't help but wonder if the studio had used Daddy's name, and set the remake in McNairy County, if the movie would have been a bigger success. That's one more question in my life that will never be answered.

CHAPTER 18

My Thoughts About Daddy's Death

Many people have their own theories about how my daddy died. Some believe that his death was simply an accident. I respect their point of view and their right to believe that. I do not choose to believe that his death was accidental. There are others who were close to my father who also took that stance. After the car crash, Papaw said, "He never lost control. Something else is wrong." And his deputy, Peatie Plunk, never bought the death scene as simply an accident. "He was a good driver. He was a fast driver but he was a good driver," Peatie said, disbelieving the official report.

While I do not believe that Larry Britt, the private investigator who conned my grandmother out of our inheritance in his "search" for my daddy's killers, was ever even remotely conducting a legitimate investigation, I do believe that my daddy's death was caused by others.

In 1990, a lawman friend of mine gave me what I believe is a major piece of the puzzle concerning what caused my daddy's death.

I have an accounting of the last few days before Daddy died. Daddy told us two weeks before his death that he knew there was a new contract being put out on his life. I also know that a man had made Daddy aware of the contract and that this same man is the one called repeatedly the day of his wreck, trying to warn him.

The man, who had been an informant for my father, talked to my grandmother and others that day—desperately

A state historical marker stands near the site where my father lost his life. (Photograph by Wiley Brewer)

trying to reach Daddy to warn him that the people with the contract were going to try to kill him that night. The man knew about the plan and knew about money being paid for it. This man had an association with those involved. In the document I received from my lawman friend, key portions of which I am about to share here, this same man tells the story about knowing firsthand of plans to kill my father. I won't name names because I fear for the safety of my family. But I know names. There are other key people who also know this information and keep their records of it in secure places.

Having taken several precautions, I finally feel comfortable telling my theory of my daddy's death without revealing any names of those who I think might have been involved. However, if anything happens to me or to my family, the names in this document will be revealed and these men will have to answer for the events of the night of August 20, 1974.

First, let me set the stage. During August 1974, Ray Blanton, an Adamsville native and the U.S. congressman representing our district, was the Democratic candidate for governor of Tennessee. Though a Republican, Daddy had agreed to campaign for Ray, whom Daddy regarded as a friend, if not exactly a close friend. The understanding that Daddy had was that, if he campaigned for Blanton and if Blanton then won the governor's seat, Daddy would be appointed Commissioner of Safety, whose domain included the Highway Patrol and, at that time but no longer, also the Tennessee Bureau of Investigation.

The Commissioner of Safety position would have given Daddy easy access to information about criminal activity, as well as the authority to act on the information in a much more substantial way than he had been able to do at the local level—even more than when he was sheriff of McNairy County. At one time, the Republicans had tried to convince Daddy to run for governor, but that office wasn't the one he wanted. He wanted to be Commissioner of Safety, where he could have had direct control of investigations.

A lot of powerful people and a lot of bad people had a reason to fear Daddy's being in a position to open old cases and devote significant manpower and other resources to investigating them. With Ray Blanton leading in the polls, their fear of Daddy may have been so great that these people thought that they couldn't take any chances. They had to kill my daddy.

The fact that Daddy had warned us to be extra careful because he had heard that there was a contract on his life is further evidence that some evil directed toward him was afoot. That fact, combined with the phone calls to our house trying to warn Daddy that "they" were going to try to kill him that night, builds a strong basis for believing that Daddy's death was not simply an accident. And especially not on the road between Selmer and Adamsville, which he knew so very well.

Daddy was driving a car that he had owned for almost a year, so I don't believe that he was unfamiliar with the car and didn't know how to handle it. Some folks claim that maybe he simply had had too much to drink. That, they say, coupled with a high rate of speed might be what caused the crash. My belief is that, yes, he may have been sipping something at times during the evening, but an intoxicated man would not have been able to win all those prizes for me at the games of skill at the county fair not long before we left the fairgrounds and headed home.

Some reports, including the official one released by General Motors after its examination of the car following the accident, concluded that the tie rods on Daddy's Corvette had not been tampered with. Maybe they weren't. But I do know that in the late 1980s, about fifteen years after Daddy's car wreck, a man from General Motors was visiting the Chevrolet dealership in Savannah, Tennessee, when I happened to drop by the dealership. After I went back to the radio station where I worked, the GM man tracked me down and said, "I just had to let you know. I was there when we did the investigation of the car. Our conclusion as to whether the tie rod was tampered with could have gone either way. It was that close. There wasn't definitive evidence either way. Rather than unnecessarily alarming Corvette owners that their cars might be easily tampered with, when we really couldn't say for sure, our report stated that there was no evidence of tampering. But I always believed in my heart that it was tampered with." I believe the GM man.

The police reports also state that there were two sets of skid marks at the accident scene, the ones from Daddy's car and another set. Was the second set of tracks just a coincidence? Had Daddy been racing someone? Had Daddy's car been forced off the road in some way? These are all unanswered questions.

Most of this evidence is largely circumstantial. But when taken in the context of the portion of the document I'm about to share, all of the pieces start to fit together into a reasonable picture of what could have happened.

This document came into my possession from a friend in

Daddy's Corvette went into a long skid crossing the oncoming westbound lane of U.S. Highway 64 about four miles west of our home in Adamsville and smashed into an embankment. Here the skid marks show that the car was traveling sideways. (Photograph by John George, *Memphis Press Scimitar,* courtesy of Mississippi Valley Collection, University of Memphis Libraries)

law enforcement who had received it from another member of law enforcement, who was investigating police corruption in Mississippi. An official discovered the document in a manila envelope fastened to the underside of a drawer in a filing cabinet in the office of someone who was being investigated about matters totally unrelated to anything involving my daddy or his death.

When the man saw that this document discussed my daddy, he passed it along to my friend, who gave the document to me. Mostly because of fear of what might happen to my family or me, I have not done anything with the document until now. But I think the time has come to share the story, but not the names of those involved. I still have enough fear for the safety of my family not to want to reveal the names.

As for the man who is making the first-person statement in the document about his activities, he was an informant for my father. His statement covers a wide range of his own criminal activities. I'll summarize some of the parts that are background and then use the man's words verbatim for the parts that pertain to my Daddy and his death. I suspect that at the time the man gave this statement he was likely going into the witness protection program, but I can't be positive about that. I don't know his current whereabouts.

Here, then, is this unidentified man's story, with Person N, Person X, etc., replacing the actual names of people. I don't want to incorrectly incriminate innocent parties to the story, and I'm also still fearful of others who may have been behind my father's death.

The man's statement describes his teenage years during the early 1960s, when he was involved in buying liquor and handguns and taking part in criminal activities, especially car theft. He tells about serving prison time in Missouri and Mississippi for car theft. He describes returning to northeastern Mississippi and developing closer contact with known criminals, including Towhead White and Person N.

He next describes living out of state, where he was involved with a girl from that area. He describes happening to meet an associate of Towhead White at a local tavern in that state, but says that he made a point of staying away from the man after riding with him to a shipyard, where the man proceeded to take a body from his trunk and dump it into a lake.

He describes being broke and trying to steal merchandise that he could then sell in order to have enough money to leave that state. But he was caught stealing the merchandise and served jail time.

He next talks about returning to northeastern Mississippi, where he painted and dismantled stolen cars for a man from 1967 to 1969.

He says that around 1969 he began working with men who were burglarizing airports. The gang would steal airplane parts and tools. They committed similar thefts at shoe factories and boat docks. It was during this time that the man learned how to fly a plane.

He describes going to Lexington, Tennessee, in July 1969 to pick up some stolen cars. He and another man towed the cars to Adamsville. "We all went to [a nearby restaurant], whereupon the [other] man who drove back from Lexington went into the restaurant and returned with a large amount of money that he had gotten from the cars."

That's the general background about the man and his way of life.

His statement continues.

I first met Buford Pusser during 1969 at the McNairy County Airport. At this time, I had drifted away from my [car-theft work] and was now . . . doing legitimate work. . . . When I first met Pusser, he offered to pay me for information about minor crimes in McNairy County, Tennessee, and surrounding areas. He said he wanted to go for a ride in the plane, which surprised me since I didn't actually have my license yet. Pusser said he knew I had gotten a raw deal from Person X and [a man in law enforcement in Mississippi] concerning some stolen goods that I bought which were intended for Person X. Person X had turned me in for stealing the goods, and [the man in law enforcement] beat me up while in the jail.

After this beating, and being released on bond, I went to McNairy County, Tennessee, to look for a man who sold me the stolen parts. Since I had told R. C. Matlock, one of Pusser's deputies, about what [the man in law enforcement] and Person X had done, I figured this was the only way Pusser could have known about the raw deal. . . .

Buford and I flew for about twenty minutes, during which time I consented to give Pusser the information he wanted, mostly because I was fed up with Person X and also because of Pusser's promise to make it worth my while. In all, up until 1970 when my contract with Pusser diminished, he

*gave me about $150 to $200 for information. Pusser and I
usually met at the state line road or near what is now the
Torch Club. My mother [and three others] were the only ones
who knew I was giving information to Pusser. . . .*

*In the spring of 1970, Pusser gave me an honorary
deputy's card, which among other things entitled me to a
cheap cup of coffee in local restaurants. If [my two criminal
associates] were aware of me having the card, it would not
have bothered them since these cards were easy to come by
and it didn't necessarily indicate a closeness with the law.
As mentioned supra, my contract diminished in the last half
of 1970, particularly after 8-31-70, the date his term as sheriff expired. At this time, I was developing an interest in law
enforcement as a result of my contract with Pusser.*

*In the latter part of 1970, I left [my job] and went
pipelining, a legitimate business, until returning to start
school . . . in the fall of 1971.*

He goes on to describe his continuing education and his
rise into high-ranking civic and law-enforcement positions
in northeastern Mississippi. He then continues with more
discussion about my daddy.

*In a conversation that nobody knows about, I told
Pusser that [a certain person], a resident of Burnsville,
had the gun that killed Pusser's wife, August 12, 1967.
[That same person] worked for [a leader of alcohol traffic
in northeastern Mississippi]. . . .*

*At this time, I did not know any of the plots to kill
Pusser, although there were always rumors around state
line joints. As mentioned in previous paragraphs, while
working in [a nearby town], I saw Pusser once, maybe
more. I felt Pusser was using me to get at criminals in [a
certain location] that would be beyond his jurisdiction,
even though at the time he was out of law enforcement.
Pusser would give me tips to help me rise politically, such
as telling me who and where to check for what.*

The man goes on to describe some of the problems relating to his job and his pursuit of his education. Some of the discussion includes politics in his town and charges of criminal activity made against him. He then continues his statement as follows:

Art Murphy was the police chief in Corinth. While I was visiting there on March 3, 1973, he was killed. [Someone] had told me earlier in the evening that Murphy would be killed. (See deposition.) And [another person] had told me to keep quiet about it. I obliged. Person H killed Murphy. But Person H was released within hours, since [local law enforcement] said it was in self-defense. Person H immediately went to Chicago upon his release. I later told my mother [and two others] what happened. Furthermore, I went to . . . the county attorney, and asked him to make me a special investigator, which he did. This angered several people in law enforcement who knew what had happened, even though I tried to brush it off as having nothing to do with Murphy's death. I believe the people responsible for Murphy's death decided I knew too much and they tried to get rid of me. More than once my murder was attempted. Once by throwing boulders from the overpass through my windshield. Also, I was shot and did chase [a certain person] home since it was [this person] whom I believe to have shot me.

During [that pursuit], I did temporarily lose control of my car and was unable to apprehend [this person]. However, I did see water returning to a mud hole in his driveway when I arrived at his residence. I also observed lights being turned off. I was off work for three days. A charge of embezzlement had already been brought against me as a result of a car I had purchased from [a person], which happened to have a county radio in it. Although I got a bill of sale, this embezzlement charge was brought in what I'm sure was in an attempt to get me back into [a certain jurisdiction], where they can deal with me.

Because of this charge and the concurrent political upheaval, I had to leave [the town where I had been living] and return to Corinth in the fall of 1973, as is mentioned supra.

News of the embezzlement charge became known, I was dropped from [my law-enforcement job], and had to quit school, due to lack of money. While in Corinth, I couldn't live at home with my mother and family because of safety reasons. I stayed at Corinth Plaza Motel and Noel Motel.

In late 1973, Pusser visited me at this motel. [Three people] should be able to attest that Pusser visited me. Also my mother and [another person] were aware of some of the meetings. Around mid-1974, I saw Pusser again at Coleman's Bar-B-Que in Corinth. This bar-b-que was and is situated on Highway 45 North at Seventh Street. It was at this time that I advised him that Person N had called me concerning splitting a contract on Pusser's death with him. Pusser told me to "stick with [it]" to see what develops. I never saw him again until the night he was killed and that was the time [August 20] he was on TV in Memphis signing a contract with some people concerning a new movie. [There are] two persons who should have seen us together during this meeting.

On July 24 or 26, 1974, I met Person N at the Thunderbird Motel [in Jackson]. I had gotten there before Person N and rented a room under the name of Jack North. At the time, I was driving my wife's car. While we were there, I met [a man I knew], who haggled with Person N about money in the parking lot. Later that night, I returned to Corinth.

About a week later, Person N and his girlfriend met me at Null Brothers garage, where he told me it was coming down soon, apparently referring to Pusser's death. Later that night, we went to a tavern in Tennessee.

On or about August 16, 1974, Person N contacted me at my mother's and we went to Katherine's Club in Tennessee to do some drinking. While there, I overheard [two men] discussing a front-end man in Memphis. They knew that Pusser was coming back from Memphis and [one man] asked [the other] if he had gotten the money together. I presume they discussed the money with Person N. We went home.

A few days later, I returned to the Thunderbird Motel in Jackson. At this time, Person N drove a green or brown '69 Chevy. While I waited in the car, Person N went to the room to get the money. I jotted down the license numbers of several cars in the parking lot. In particular, I remember spotting [a certain man's] car. When Person N returned to the car, he had $10,000 and said [four men known to me] and a man from California were in the room. Incidentally, Person N had a set of GM master keys, explosives, rope, tools, front-end parts, etc., in his car while we made this trip. He told me that, when it was over, he would split the money with me.

On August 20, 1974, Person N called me and said to meet him at Eastview, Tennessee, in McNairy County, at 6 or 8 P.M. He said it was going to happen between Colliersville and Adamsville. I did not go to Eastview. Rather, I tried to contact Pusser, who I knew was in Memphis. My [girlfriend] and I called every Holiday Inn in Memphis, as well as the McNairy County sheriff's office and Pusser's parents, but could not reach him. One of these calls, I did identify myself, McNairy County [sheriff's office]. Later I saw Person N in Corinth after Pusser's death and he wanted to know what happened to me. I brushed it off saying something had come up and I couldn't make it. We had some drinks and seemingly the matter was forgotten.

Approximately the same time, our trailer was shot up and [my girlfriend] went to the hospital with her nerves. Her doctor advised her to get out of that stupid town before she had a nervous breakdown. After these incidents, we left for Mexico, where [my girlfriend] got a divorce from her husband on or about 4-30-75.

After a while, we returned to Corinth and then left for

Florida, where we were married 6-12-75. While in Florida,
I learned that Person N had been killed by [another man].
[The investigator] claims that Person N came to kill [the
man] due to remarks made about Person N's sex habits
and that [the man] had acted in self-defense. I know that
the substance of these alleged remarks [was] untrue and I
believe that it is a fact that Person N's gun was never fired.
Since learning of Person N's death, we have been on the
run ever since.

It is my belief that those people who had Person N killed
also want me silenced because I know too much.

So there's the man's statement that was passed along to
me in 1990. Though I've blurred the identities of most of the
people to a great extent, the gist of the man's statement is
crystal clear. He states that there was an active plot under
way to kill my father on a roadway and it was to be done on
the very day that he ended up being killed.

Is this man's story truthful or just total baloney? I can't
say with complete certainty. But I know of no reason why
this person would lie about this. His statement reads as an
attempt to set the record straight and come clean about the
many missteps in his own life.

The story he tells fits well with other facts from my
daddy's life and the bits of information that others and I
have pieced together about the day he died. I think this is
the key missing piece of the puzzle concerning how my
daddy died.

Beneath the cloaking of names in this story are powerful
people, bad people, and powerful bad people. Do I think the
plot described above and my daddy's death are a coincidence?

No way.

If this man's statement is true, then some of the conspir-
ators in my daddy's murder are still free and have never
faced justice. Though this is just one man's statement, it
does raise serious questions about the circumstances of my

daddy's death. That the allegations in the man's statement have never, to my knowledge, been investigated by law enforcement is curious. But then, I too have been reluctant to pursue the allegations and the people mentioned, because of fear for the safety of my family and me. Preserving personal safety versus pursuing truth and justice—it's a tough struggle for me.

I have chosen safety for my family and me. But if that safety is ever threatened, I've made sure that truth and justice will be sought—with a vengeance.

EPILOGUE

There have been times, while writing about my life, that I have felt great anxiety both about bringing up painful memories and sharing so much of my pain and my life with an unknown world. At times I have felt a renewed loneliness for my parents—a sadness not only for myself but for my children, who never got to know their grandparents.

As I have reflected on the years of my life so far, I've been grateful for the strong influence my grandmother had in my life. It has made me reevaluate and appreciate her that much more. Taking on the raising of a teenager couldn't have been easy at her age.

There have been some really hard issues that I have had to address with this book. On a day-to-day basis, I don't dwell on those issues. I don't routinely go back to painful times and places, because I know I need to keep walking forward. I don't go back unless pressed. For this book, I have had to go back. It has been both good and bad.

In compiling my thoughts for this book, I became amazed at even getting to this point at my life. I've lived well past the ages of my parents. I seem to be the lone survivor of the Pusser bunch.

It also amazes and surprises me that I'm as sane as I am. I don't know why it is that I've got a lick of sense. (Maybe I don't.) I just hope that one day my children and my grandchildren appreciate what my daddy did for our community and our county, as well as the impact he has had across the

Ned Ray McWherter, left, was a huge help in getting the state of Tennessee to turn our former home into a museum when he was Speaker of the House. To the right of Daddy in this 1973 photo are Lt. Gov. John Wilder and U.S. Congressman Robin Beard.

state, the country, and the world. I get notes and e-mails every day from folks telling me about the effect he has had on their lives. That continues to amaze me and touch my heart.

I'm always proud of Daddy, but never has my respect for him been greater than while I was working on this project. As I look at how young he was during all of these incredible events, I can't even begin to comprehend how he dealt with the situations he faced. As young as he was, he had a big burden on his shoulders as he tried to tackle the state line gang and other problems. When there are dark times and I feel as though I can't make it another day, I just remember Daddy. I remind myself that part of him is in me. I realize I can do whatever it takes to meet the challenges I face and keep . . . *walking on.*

APPENDIX A

Buford Pusser Festival

The City of Adamsville held a Buford Pusser Day in October of 1973, the year before Daddy was killed. Daddy participated. There are mementos from that day, including the referee shirt that he wore for a wrestling match that was staged as part of that celebration. After Daddy died, there were no more official celebrations of his life until the museum was dedicated in 1987.

The Town of Adamsville Business and Professional Association held an arts and crafts day in the spring each year. When we were getting ready to open the museum, the association decided to hold its crafts fair on Memorial Day weekend. We tied the museum's ribbon-cutting ceremony in with it and had a big parade. The next year, a carnival was added in what is now Buford Pusser Park. The third year, the event became the Buford Pusser Festival, which is held each Memorial Day weekend.

The Law Enforcement Officer of the Year Award has become the centerpiece of the festival. We also honor law-enforcement officers who have been killed in the line of duty.

There's a 5K run, car show, antique tractor show, and motorcycle show. My daddy would have loved all those vehicles. The weekend also includes a celebrity golf tournament and entertainment by various country music, bluegrass, and gospel performers from Nashville and elsewhere.

The festival draws about five thousand people, which is a comfortable number for a town the size of Adamsville—big enough to make the festival feel like a "happening" and not so big that the event loses its small-town feel. The festival is established enough now that it's able to raise some money to help maintain the museum through the Buford Pusser Foundation.

I'm proud that a festival that bears Daddy's name can be a positive thing for the community. It's a fun event for people in Adamsville and also promotes tourism. The salutes to law enforcement are especially poignant for me. The weekend has an underlying purpose that's serious, but mostly it's fun. Y'all come!

Learn more about the festival, the museum, and other topics pertaining to the legend of Buford Pusser on the Web at www.sheriffbufordpusser.com.

APPENDIX B

The Death of Buford Pusser

Here is a portion of Tennessee Highway Patrol Trooper Paul Ervin's accident report, followed by some witness statements. Some witnesses recalled a few details differently, but together they provide insight into what occurred that night.

Describe what happened:
Vehicle #1 traveling east on Highway 64. Driver of vehicle #1 lost control. Vehicle went into a skid, skidded approximately 345 feet crossing the westbound lane, left the road, skidded 200 feet across loose gravel on front of old Shell station and across Lawton Road. Vehicle #1 then struck the road bank on the east side of Lawton Road. Vehicle #1 then continued on approximately 40 feet in a southeast direction landing on the wheels. Driver was thrown from vehicle and landed approximately 3 feet to the rear of the vehicle. Vehicle was headed to the north. Vehicle then caught fire and burned.

Investigation of a 10:46 involving Buford H. Pusser
Trooper Paul Ervin, Aug. 23, 1974
Approximately 12:00 A.M., Aug. 21, 1974, I was dispatched to a 10:46, 7 miles east of Selmer.
Approximately 1 mile before I reached the scene, flames and a set of blue lights were visible.
At approximately 12:05 A.M., I arrived at the scene and found a vehicle burning and a body laying approximately

100 feet east of the burning vehicle. Also, T.W. Burks of the Adamsville Police, Danny Browder, Jason Hollingsworth and Dwana Pusser were there.

Talking to Danny Browder, who was the first to discover the wreck, he said he heard the vehicle and the crash. His statement was that it sounded like a jet. Browder was watching T.V. and went outside to see if he could see anything and said that he could not see anything in any direction so he got in his vehicle and stated that it might be over the hill. Starting to leave he saw the vehicle and a body laying behind the vehicle close to the road, and that there was a small fire under the hood. Browder said that he knew that he needed help and went back to the house to call for help. After calling for help he returned to the scene to find Jason Hollingsworth and Dwana Pusser, who had moved the body approximately 100 feet east of the burning vehicle. Dwana Pusser was saying to Burks and Hollingsworth that Daddy was dead and she wanted to go home. She was upset.

Jason Hollingsworth said that he and Pusser had come from the McNairy County Fair and that they were not close enough to see the accident. Hollingsworth said that night that Pusser had passed him coming from the fair and would not make any comment as to how fast the vehicle might have been going, but later he said that a car passed him at a high rate of speed and that he was not sure that it was Pusser, but that Dwana Pusser thought it was her father. Hollingsworth said he did not meet or was not passed by any other vehicle from that time till he came to the wreck.

The ambulance called by Officer Burks arrived driven by Don Smith.

The Medical Examiner, Dr. Harry L. Peeler was called to the scene to make his investigation. After Dr. Peeler made his examination, the body was carried to the McNairy County General Hospital.

After the fire died down, a wrecker was called at Trooper's request. Joe Burkeen's Texaco of Bethel Springs was called by dispatcher to remove the vehicle and store it.

Statement of Mr. Dennie Howell
Selmer, Tennessee
8-22-74 5:30 PM
To Trooper Paul Ervin

I told Mr. Howell that I understood that he had seen Mr. Pusser at the McNairy County Fair and would he tell me anything that he knew about Mr. Pusser's condition.

Mr. Howell stated that he saw Mr. Pusser at the fair along with his niece Angie Lock. It was about 10:45 PM on Aug. 20, 1974. While talking with him he seemed to be stuttering more than usual, and as we walked away, my niece said she thought that she smelled liquor, and he was drinking something out of a Coleman's Bar-B-Que cup.

Statement Miss Angie Lock
Selmer, Tennessee
8-23-74 6:00 PM
To Trooper Paul Ervin

Tell me what you know about Buford Pusser's condition on the night of his wreck. What did you smell about him?

I smelled something and thought it was alcohol. He was drinking something out of a cup, a Coleman's Bar-B-Que cup.

Statement of Mr. Bennie Gaines
Owner of Coleman's Bar-B-Que
Selmer, Tennessee
8-23-74 6:02 PM

Mr. Gaines stated that on the night of Aug. 20-74, Mr. Pusser came in and ordered two large Bar-B-Ques and a large glass of water. He returned in a few minutes and ordered a fish sandwich and another large cup of water.

I did not detect the odor of alcohol or see any effects of alcohol.

Statement of Mr. Roger Horton
River Heights Restaurant
8-21-74 6:50 PM
To Sgt. Gerald Allen

Mr. Horton was asked if he had any knowledge of the accident that we could use in our investigation, reference to his statement on television.

Mr. Horton stated that he was just a close personal friend of Mr. Pusser and that they had went to school together, and that he had rode in the car with Mr. Pusser many times. He believed that Mr. Pusser was just too good a driver for that to happen.

Also that Mr. Pusser had asked him in the past, that if anything like this ever happened to him, to try to check it out. Mr. Horton said that he was not trying to do anyone's job for them, but just didn't want anyone to do that to Mr. Pusser and get away with it.

Asked what he was basing his opinion on that the tie-rod end was out or filed?

Mr. Horton stated that it just looked that way to him, that he was not an expert on it, but it did look that way to him. He also stated that he was not a mechanic or had any experience in that line.

The main point that he stressed to me was that he did not want anyone to get away with killing Mr. Pusser, if that's what happened. He then stated that if it was just an accident, then he would be satisfied with that.

Statement Mrs. Gail Davis
Buford Pusser's sister
8-22-74 1:30 PM
To Sgt. Gerald Allen

Called Pusser residence to see if Miss Dwana Pusser was able to talk with me and give any information about the accident. Mrs. Gail Davis, Buford Pusser's sister, answered the phone and requested that we did not attempt to talk to Miss Pusser as she had been very upset and did not feel up to talking to anyone.

I advised Mrs. Davis that I did not want to bother her, that I just wanted to know if she had seen anything that might help our investigation, as she had stated on television that she had seen the vehicle leave the road and hit the bank.

Mrs. Davis then told me that the news people had gotten everything mixed up about that, that Miss Pusser was behind Mr. Pusser in another vehicle, but that she definitely did not see the accident. It had already happened when they drove up, and Mr. Pusser was out of the vehicle lying on the ground. Miss Pusser said the vehicle was not on fire at that time, and that Mr. Pusser tried to say his daughter's name twice and that was all.

Statement Mr. Don Maxedon
Selmer, Tennessee
8-22-74 7:00 PM
To Sgt. Gerald Allen and Trooper Paul Ervin

We told Mr. Maxedon that we understood that he was one of the last people to see Mr. Pusser before the accident and we would like for him to tell us anything that he could about it.

Mr. Maxedon stated that he talked to Mr. Pusser while he was shooting basketball, and that he didn't see anything wrong with him. He also said that he didn't smell any alcohol on him or any effect of it.

Mr. Maxedon also said that they were parked next to Mr. Pusser's car, and that he noticed that Mr. Pusser went to his car and sat in it and was talking to his daughter and eating two Bar-B-Que sandwiches. He said they sat there talking for 15 or 20 minutes and that Buford started his car and pulled out fast, spinning the wheels on his car. Another vehicle pulled up, and Dwana got in it, and they left behind Buford, in about 60 seconds or a minute or so.

Statement Mr. Carroll Bodiford
Selmer, Tennessee
8-22-74 5:45 PM
To Sgt. Gerald Allen and Trooper Paul Ervin

We told Mr. Bodiford that we understood that he was one of the last people to see Mr. Pusser before the accident, and we would like for him to tell us anything that he could about it.

Mr. Bodiford stated that he saw Mr. Pusser at the McNairy County Fair shooting basketball. When he spoke to Mr. Pusser he didn't have much to say. Something was definitely wrong, he was in a quiet, non-talkative mood. He wasn't right, don't know for sure whether he was drinking or not, but something was wrong.

When we started to leave we were parked close to him, but the closest I got to him was across the car. Buford did leave at a pert speed, had that Corvette gurgling, going fast like a teenager.

APPENDIX C

Film and TV Credits

Here are production credits for the *Walking Tall* movies and TV series.

WALKING TALL
Filmed in 1972; released on February 22, 1973

Directed by Phil Karlson
Written by Mort Briskin and Stephen Downing
Starring Joe Don Baker as Buford Pusser, Elizabeth Hartman as Pauline Pusser, Gene Evans as Sheriff Al Thurman, Noah Beery, Jr., as Grandpa Carl Pusser, Brenda Benet as Luan Paxton, John Brascia as Prentiss Parley, Bruce Glover as Grady Coker, Arch Johnson as Buel Jaggers, Felton Perry as Obra Eaker, Richard X. Slattery as Arno Purdy, Rosemary Murphy as Callie Hacker, Lynn Borden as Margie Ann, Ed Call as Lutie McVeigh, Sidney Clute as Sheldon Levine, Douglas Fowley as Judge R. W. Clarke, Don Keefer as Dr. Lamar Stivers, Sam Laws as Willie Rae Lockman, Pepper Martin as Zolan Dicks, John Myhers as Lester Dickens, Logan Ramsey as John Witter, Kenneth Tobey as Augie McCullah, Lurene Tuttle as Grandma Pusser, Leif Garrett as Mike Pusser, Dawn Lyn as Dwana Pusser, Dominick Mazzie as Bozo, Russell Thorson as Ferrin Meaks, Gil Perkins as bouncer, Carey Loftin as dice player, Warner Venetz as Stickman, Gene Le Bell as bouncer, Del Monroe

as Otie Doss, Lloyd Tatum as prosecutor, Vaudie Plunk as jury foreman, Pearline Wynn as Hassie Berlson, Ted Jordan as Virgil Burton, Red West as Sheriff Tanner, Andrew J. Pirtle as prisoner, Lloyd Harris as doctor in the emergency room (uncredited), and Chris Ladd as bar patron (uncredited)
Executive producer Charles A. Pratt
Producer Mort Briskin
Associate producer Joel Briskin
Original music by Walter Scharf, lyricist Don Black
Stunt coordinators Carey Loftin and Gil Perkins
Stunt double for Joe Don Baker, Roydon Clark (uncredited)
Technical advisor Buford Pusser

WALKING TALL—PART II
Released on July 2, 1975

Directed by Earl Bellamy
Written by Howard B. Kreitsek
Starring Bruce Glover as Grady Coker, Bo Svenson as Buford Pusser, Robert DoQui as Obra Eaker, Noah Beery, Jr., as Carl Pusser, Archie Grinalds as A. C. Hand, Allen Mullikin as Floyd Tate, Logan Ramsey as John Witter, Luke Askew as Pinky Dobson, John Davis Chandler as Ray Henry, Lloyd Tatum as FBI agent, Lurene Tuttle as Grandma Pusser, Dawn Lyn as Dwana Pusser, Leif Garrett as Mike Pusser, Libby Boone as Joan Lashley, Jimmy Moore as Miles, Richard Jaeckel as Stud Pardee, Brooke Mills as Ruby Ann, Frank McRae as Steamer Riley, William Bryant as FBI agent, Gary M. Darling as Rudy, Angel Tompkins as Marganne Stillson, Levi Frazier, Jr., as runaway moonshiner, Red West as Sheriff Tanner, Jon R. Wilson as lumber-truck driver, Ken Zimmerman as water-truck driver, and Chris Ladd as deputy (uncredited)
Producer Charles A. Pratt
Original music by Walter Scharf
Stunts by Carey Loftin

WALKING TALL—THE FINAL CHAPTER
1977

Directed by Jack Starrett
Written by Howard B. Kreitsek and Samuel A. Peeples
Starring Bo Svenson as Buford Pusser, Margaret Blye as Luan, Forrest Tucker as Grandpa Pusser, Morgan Woodward as The Boss, Libby Boone as Pusser's secretary, David Adams as Robbie Teal, Vance Davis as Aaron, Leif Garrett as Mike Pusser, Bruce Glover as Deputy Grady, H. B. Haggerty as Bulow, Taylor Lacher as Martin French, Dawn Lyn as Dwana Pusser, John Malloy as producer, Sandy McPeak as Lloyd Tatum, Robert Phillips as Johnny, Logan Ramsey as John Witter, Clay Tanner as O. Q. Teal, Lurene Tuttle as Grandma Pusser, Wanda Wilson as Betty, and Chris Ladd as newspaper photographer (uncredited)
Producer Charles A. Pratt
Original music by Walter Scharf
Stunt coordinator Paul Nuckles
Stunts by Russ McCubbin (uncredited)

A REAL AMERICAN HERO
1978 TV movie

Directed by Lou Antonio
Written by Samuel A. Peeples
Starring Brian Dennehy as Buford Pusser, Forrest Tucker as Carl Pusser, Brian Kerwin as Til Johnson, Ken Howard as Danny Boy Mitchell, Sheree North as Carrie Todd, Lane Bradbury as Debbie Pride, Brad David as Mick Rogers, Edward Call as Grady Coker, W. O. Smith as Obra Eaker, Julie Thrasher as Dwana Pusser, Jason Hood as Mike Pusser, Ann Street as Grandma Pusser, George Boyd as Lloyd Tatum, Maureen Burns as Amelia Biggins, Charlie Briggs as Miles Conway, and Elizabeth Lane as Sabrina Marlowe
Producer Samuel A. Peeples
Charles A. Pratt executive producer

Original music by Don Black and Walter Scharf
"Walking Tall" sung by Don Williams

"WALKING TALL"
1978 NBC TV series; seven one-hour episodes

Directed by John Florea
Written by Lee Sheldon
Starring Bo Svenson as Sheriff Buford Pusser, Rad Daly as
Michael Pusser, Heather McAdams as Dwana Pusser, Walter
Barnes as Carl Pusser, Harold Sylvester as Deputy Aaron
Fairfax, Jeff Lester as Deputy Grady Spooner, and Courtney
Pledger as Deputy Joan Litton
Executive producer David Gerber
Producer Mel Swope
Stunts by Dean Raphael Ferrandini and Leslie Hoffman

WALKING TALL
2004

Directed by Kevin Bray
Written by (earlier) Mort Briskin, David Klass, Channing
Gibson, David Levien, and Brian Koppelman
Starring The Rock as Chris Vaughn, Johnny Knoxville as
Ray Templeton, Neal McDonough as Jay Hamilton, Kristen
Wilson as Michelle Vaughn, Ashley Scott as Deni, Khleo
Thomas as Pete Vaughn, John Beasley as Chris Vaughn, Sr.,
Barbara Tarbuck as Connie Vaughn, Michael Bowen as
Sheriff Stan Watkins, Kevin Durand as Booth, Andrew
Tarbet as Jimmy, Patrick Gallagher as Keith, John Stewart
as Rusty, Eric Breker as Deputy Ralston, Ryan Robbins as
Travis, Michael Adamthwaite as Burke, Darcy Laurie as
Smitty, Fred Keating as doctor, Ben Cardinal as Michelle's
partner, Kett Turton as Kenner, Terence Kelly as Judge L.
Powell, Tom Scholte as attorney Merle Crowe, Mark
Houghton as county prosecutor, James Ashcroft as bailiff

Producers Ashok Amritraj, Bill Bannerman, Jim Burke, Lucas Foster, Marcienne Friesland, David Hoberman, Keith Samples, and Paul Schiff
Original music by Graeme Revell
Dedicated to Buford Pusser